WHAT GREAT PARENTS DO

75

Simple Strategies for
Raising Kids Who
Thrive

ERICA REISCHER, PHD

A TarcherPerigee Book

tarcherperigee

An imprint of Penguin Random House LLC
375 Hudson Street
New York, New York 10014

ISBN 9780399176692

Printed in the United States of America
1 3 5 7 9 10 8 6 4 2

For R, my best friend and partner in all things
For A, C, and children everywhere, my why
With thanks to LB, for innumerable contributions

Contents

Introduction

WHEN I BECAME a parent, I wanted to find a book that would summarize, with an eye toward action steps, all the parenting "best practices" I had read about as a psychology graduate student.

I was able to find concise guidebooks for children's physical health, but in the broad area of children's social and emotional development, the best offerings were informative but required reading hundreds of pages in order to extract the most useful ideas, or they were overly focused in their subject matter.

After my first child was born and I started a private practice, I developed a workshop for parents that offered exactly what I had been looking for when I became a parent. Also called "What Great Parents Do," the workshop presents simply and concisely the best practices—synthesized from research and clinical experience—that help parents reshape kids' challenging behavior, create strong family bonds, and guide children toward becoming happy, kind, and responsible adults. By now, thousands of parents have attended these workshops, and they continue to this day.

The workshops were also inspired by another source. As a psychologist, I work with a variety of families, ranging from those seeking help to curb power struggles or habitual whining to those whose relationships with each other have deteriorated to such an extent that they need professional help.

Working with these families raised a broader question for me: If I could give parents critical information early in their parenting life that would help them get and stay on track to having a happy family life and raising kids who thrive, what would I tell them? The workshops, and now this book, are based on my answer to that question.

What Makes This Book Different

When I originally developed the workshop, I also created a simple one-page handout, called "10 Things Great Parents Do," summarizing ten of the key ideas presented in the workshop. Parents were welcome to share this handout with friends and family, and it has since traveled far and wide. I've received e-mails from across the country written by parents thanking me for the insights and reminders and telling me the handout is now posted on their refrigerator.

The format of this book was inspired by the many requests I've received for more action-oriented summaries of parenting best practices. I've also included real examples and practical tips for each parenting practice (aka strategy) in the book, just as I do in the live workshops.

In contrast to the many parenting books that you must read or skim hundreds of pages in order to extract the highlights and useful ideas, this book is intended to be more like a practical manual: concise and easy to read, with a focus on useful strategies you can implement right away.

For that reason, I call these "simple strategies" because they are presented in a straightforward and pared down way while still giving you enough information to translate them into action. But *simple* is not always *easy*: Although each strategy has been crafted to be easily understood, actually doing something in a different way than how we have done it in the past can be difficult. Intention and practice are key (see #2).

In this book, you will learn all the information and techniques that I teach in my workshops and private practice: previews, power sharing, pivoting, reframing, empathy, replays, fair warning, stopping the action, social experiments, reward economies, emotion coaching, happiness habits, and more—plus how to combine them in powerful ways to create the family life you want. You will learn how to manage challenging behavior like whining and procrastinating without nagging or yelling, and how to help your children become responsible stewards of their own lives.

The strategies in this book apply to children of all ages. That said, my goal here is to help parents build a strong foundation for a happy family life with thriving kids, so the ideas, approaches, and examples presented here are primarily directed at children's first ten years. But it's never too late to start (see #75). For parents of older children, it may be more challenging but well worth the effort. We are always building relationships with our children, whether they are two or twenty-two years old.

Why a practical manual? As a psychologist, I have found that most of my patients—indeed, most of the people I know, including myself—agree in principle with advice such as, "To protect your lower back, strengthen your core muscles" or "To minimize investment risk, diversify your portfolio," but aren't always able to put those ideas into practice because, in many cases, they don't yet know *how*. They think to themselves, "Yes, good idea, I want to do that, but exactly *how* do I do it?"

Similarly, in my work with families, I have found that parents want to use the principles I teach, but may not know exactly how to implement them. For this reason, each strategy in the book ends with a special section ("Try This") to give you specific ideas for how to use it in your family, including step-by-step guidance and real-life examples of what to say and do.

Who This Book Is For

This book is for you if you are a new parent, about to become one, or even if you have been around the parenting block a few times. It is also for grandparents, teachers, and caregivers. It is for anyone who has kids in their life and wants a concise guidebook with concrete ideas and practical tools to ease the everyday challenges of life with kids, while also supporting children's social and emotional development.

If you feel too tired or busy to read a book (like many parents), this book is most definitely for you. Unlike a typical chapter book that you must read in order to extract the nuggets of information you can use, this book distills them for you.

How to Use This Book

You don't need to read this book from cover to cover in order to glean the highlights and practical tips. As with a guidebook, you can easily skim or browse through it to find what is most relevant to you, and return to it as a reference anytime.

Each parenting practice or strategy is presented prominently at the top of the page, accompanied by an explanation, detailed example, and "Try This" section showing you how to implement it in your life.

Because real life is complex, most of the strategies in the book are cross-referenced with each other. When there is another strategy in the book related to the one you are reading, the book will direct you to it and show you how to combine them in powerful ways using scenarios from everyday life. In this way, you can build your parenting toolbox based on what is most helpful to you right now.

Since the purpose of this book is to distill the most useful information about parenting into bite-sized summaries and examples, it is intentionally brief. For more tips, tools, and examples, please visit www.DrEricaR.com.

The ABCs of Great Parenting

Having given you a sense of what to expect in the book, I'll also say a few words about the philosophy that guides it. My recipe for great parenting is twofold. On one hand, it depends on cultivating awareness—specifically, nonjudgmental awareness—of yourself, of others (such as your family), and of the moment. What is called for with one child in one moment may not be the right approach at a different time or with a different child. As both moods and circumstances change, we need to be aware of what is happening and what is called for, and then flexibly adapt our strategy and approach.

If, for example, we have had a conflict with a coworker earlier in the day, then we need to be aware of how that conflict may still be affecting us when we arrive home for the evening, so that we don't suddenly find ourselves losing our temper. If we are feeling lonely or depressed, we need to be watchful of inadvertently putting our needs before our children's in inappropriate ways. We need to be aware of our thoughts and feelings so that we can pause, reflect, and make a *choice* about what to do, rather than simply reacting (see #11, 15, and 18).

In addition to awareness, great parenting is also grounded in what good research tells us about what works with kids. Some of this research has led to unexpected insights. Take praise, for example: It seems intuitive that the more you praise a child, the more confident the child will become. In fact, the opposite tends to be true. Children who receive excessive praise, especially nonspecific praise that is based on traits and abilities (such as "Good job" or "You're so smart") rather than effort, tend to be less confident in their abilities. (See #42 for why this is so.) Good research helps us get clear on what really works with kids and what doesn't, so that we aren't accidentally misled by ideas or theories that seem like good ideas but really aren't.

Great parenting is not about memorizing a set of rules, it's more like skillfully speaking a language. Through practice, fluent speakers internalize a set of principles and are then able to craft their language to suit the moment and their purpose. Like speaking a language, parenting is a skill that can be improved through learning and practice (see also #5). So when we combine some general principles based on research with our own moment-to-moment awareness, we can be most prepared for the parenting challenges that come our way.

Underlying the parenting practices described in this book are three key principles that I call the ABCs of great parenting. The *A* stands for Acceptance, *B* for Boundaries, and *C* for Consistency.*

The core idea behind the principle of Acceptance is that you should always communicate to your kids (through your words, behavior, and demeanor) that you love them *just the way they are* (even when you don't like their behavior or choices). Acceptance is similar to unconditional love, though I would argue that the kind of acceptance I am speaking of here is actually more challenging.

Think, for example, of a bookish and uncoordinated boy whose athletic father had always hoped for a son like himself. While this father may encourage his son to participate in sports in order to build his skills and expand his comfort zone, can the father do so in a way that still conveys love and appreciation for his son as he is, rather than disappointment at his son's failure to be what his father had hoped? This is a difficult, but vitally important, task. Some of the parenting practices that exemplify the principle of Acceptance are #6, 8, 9, 14, 16, 18, 29, 34, 39, 43, and 74.

Establishing and communicating clear Boundaries is the second key principle. Kids need limits and boundar-

---

* Please note that the parenting practices in this book related to consequences are primarily intended for use with children over age two. If you have an infant or toddler, avoid consequences in favor of supervision and redirection, and focus on building a warm and affectionate relationship. Key practices for parenting infants and toddlers comprise: #1, 8, 19, 21, 29, 30, 31, 39, 57, 58, 61, 63, 65, 67, 68, 69, 70, 71, 72, 73, and 74.

ies. They ultimately feel safest in a family environment where expectations and rules are clear and reasonable. Parenting practices that fall under the principle of Boundaries consist of #11, 21, 22, 23, 38, 41, 50, 51, 52, 71, and 72.

Strongly related to the principle of Boundaries is the principle of Consistency. Consistency means doing what you say you will do; it means being predictable. With consistency, testing of boundaries is minimized since children will quickly learn that you can be expected to follow through. Without consistency, the effectiveness of rules and boundaries is greatly reduced.

In my workshops, I sometimes use the concept of gravity to illustrate the principle of Consistency. If, when you dropped something, it occasionally (or even once) did not fall down, you might keep dropping things to see if and when it would happen again. Kids whose parents are inconsistent will generally keep testing their parents' limits and boundaries, since it's part of learning how Mom and Dad work (see #34), and the kids might also get away with it. Some parenting practices associated with the principle of Consistency are #1, 17, 18, 23, 31, 46, 47, 53, 54, and 71.

The title of the book was also carefully chosen to reflect the philosophy of parenting presented here. First, I use the word "great" to describe the kind of parenting I think we should aspire to, instead of "perfect." Perfect parents do not exist, and trying to be one of those mythical creatures is likely to invite feelings of frustration and inadequacy. Great parents make mistakes (see #12). Making mistakes can be a good thing when it gives parents the opportunity to model for kids what to do when they've made a mistake, and how to respond with integrity and responsibility.

I also deliberately titled the book "What Great Parents Do" instead of "What Great Parents Know." The difference between doing and knowing is a critical one. While we generally cannot "do" without first knowing, if we know but do not act on what we know, then change will not happen.

We have each experienced examples of this: We know we should prioritize sleep, but instead we stay up late watching movies. We know we shouldn't check our e-mail or Facebook page one more time (again), but we do. We know we should be patient with our kids, but we aren't. One of the keys to being a great parent, then, is not just knowing how, but actually *doing* what we know.

Actually doing what we know takes effort and practice (see #2). It is not easy, for example, to get up and go exercise when we really don't feel like doing it. We *know* it's the right thing to do and we also know how, but it's difficult to actually bring ourselves to *do* it. That said, once we have worked hard (effort) to get ourselves into a regular exercise routine (practice), it is much easier to maintain. For this reason, though loving our children comes naturally, parenting well is a skill that can be learned, practiced, and improved.

If we have been lucky enough to grow up with skillful parents, then we have probably acquired a good sense about what great parents do. But if, as is the case for many of us, we did not have such luck, then we need to find ways to learn and practice the skills that will help us be loving and effective parents. Even if we did have skillful parents, we can likely still improve our parenting skills, since research is continually providing new and useful insights into children's brains and behavior.

Seeing parenting as a skill also helps us to refrain from judging ourselves harshly when we make mistakes, to maintain an attitude of openness and learning, and to continually seek new and useful information in our effort to keep building our skills. So we need to know *what* to do and *how* to do it, and then we must actually go ahead and *do* it.

As you read this book—whether from cover to cover or just dipping in and out—you might find yourself experiencing feelings of dismay or even anxiety about your own parenting missteps (which we all have), such as situations you wish you had handled differently or things you wish you had known. If that's the case, please remember that we all make mistakes, our kids are resilient, and we can create change only by starting now, in this moment, to consciously choose how we want to respond to the people and events in our lives (see #75).

I'll end with a short anecdote that further illustrates my approach to great parenting. About fifteen years ago, my husband and I decided to adopt a puppy. Neither of us had ever had a dog before but we saw others doing it, it looked fun, and we both liked dogs. So we went to the local pound and brought home an adorable puppy. We quickly realized that we needed some guidance to manage all the various puppy behaviors we were dealing with daily, so we signed up for a dog-training class.

We went to the class, eager to learn how to train our dog and change some of the problematic behaviors we had noticed. As it turned out, the puppy-training class was less about training the puppy and more about training us: how to think like a dog, how to interpret dog behavior, and how to interact with the puppy in a way that would allow her to learn and grow.

Most importantly, we learned that in order to get our dog to change her behavior, we had to change ours first. This is a lesson we can apply to all our relationships. While it's tempting to look at what our children do wrong and see the solution as "fixing" our kids, that approach ignores a key principle of change in relationships.

Relationships are like a dance. If one person changes his steps, the other person must also change hers. This is especially true with our children. So the next time you find yourself wishing your kids would whine less, listen more, and so on—remember that to change your kids' behavior, you have to start by changing yourself.

Great parents

do what they say they are going to do

THIS PRINCIPLE IS twofold:

1. Don't make rules you can't or won't enforce.
2. Keep your commitments.

It's important for kids to know that you mean what you say. This builds mutual trust and respect, which are the cornerstones of a great parent–child relationship (see also #74).

So if you tell your toddler that you will leave the grocery store if she pulls one more item off the shelf, then you must be prepared to follow through (see also #53). Similarly, if your five-year-old intentionally scampers away after you tell him that he cannot go to the baseball game unless he puts his coat and shoes on right now, then the baseball game must be skipped. (But first be sure he really heard your request; see #29.)

Doing what you say you will do also has the pleasant side effect of minimizing how much testing of boundaries your kids will do. If they expect you to do what you say you will do—that is, you are predictable—then it becomes not worth their time and effort to see if you really mean it (see also #34).

For the same reason, it's equally important to keep your commitments. If you tell your child you will get off your computer in five minutes to read to him, for example, then be prepared to stop at that time and follow through on what you said. If you keep putting him off or changing the timeline ("Just a few more minutes, honey"), your child may eventually become skeptical when you make a commitment to him.

TRY THIS: Pay careful attention to the commitments you make to your kids, whether you are committing to do something together ("I'll play basketball with you after I finish this e-mail") or specifying a consequence for breaking a rule ("If you take something else off the shelf without asking, we are leaving the grocery store").

Be sure to follow through on what you've said (or acknowledge your commitment and explain carefully the reasons why you could not follow through).

2

Great parents

do what they know

ONE OF THE keys to creating positive change in our lives is not just knowing what to do, but in actually doing what we know.

The difference between knowing and doing is a critical one. While we generally cannot "do" without first knowing how to do it, if we know but do not act on what we know, change will not happen.

All of us have experienced examples of this: We know we shouldn't eat a whole carton of ice cream, but we do it anyway. We know we should exercise regularly, but we don't. We know we shouldn't yell at our kids, but we do.

Doing what we know takes both effort and practice. It is not easy to get up and go exercise when we really don't feel like doing it. It's definitely not easy to stop ourselves from yelling when it seems like our kids are ignoring us or being disrespectful.

We often know what is the right thing to do, but it can be difficult to bring ourselves to do it (or not to do what we want to avoid). Sometimes this is because we don't know exactly *how* to do what we know, and sometimes it's because we aren't taking the final step into action. Sometimes it's because we aren't yet skilled at emotion regulation (see #32), so our feelings dictate our actions (see #11).

Ultimately, we need to know *what* to do, we need to know *how* to do it, and then we need to *do* what we know. This is the three-step recipe for change.

TRY THIS: If you find yourself needing to create change, whether in your parenting life or elsewhere, ask yourself these questions to pinpoint where you need to focus:

1. Knowing what and how: Is this an issue of my not knowing what to do or how to do it?

For example, if your child is refusing to brush his teeth, do you know how to address this situation (in a way that isn't forceful—e.g., holding him down while you brush his teeth—or punitive)?

2. Doing it: Am I feeling stuck because I know what to do and how to do it, but I'm not yet putting that knowledge into practice?

This inertia often happens because we tend to be creatures of habit, so it's difficult to change our response to familiar situations. Ask yourself: What needs to happen in order for me to translate my knowledge into action?

For example, if you know how to get your children to be responsive without nagging or yelling (this book will show you how), are you putting these ideas into practice or are you still responding with old patterns of behavior?

To paraphrase Henry Ford: If you do what you've always done, you'll get what you've always gotten. To create change in your life, you must *do* something differently.

3

Great parents
change themselves first

AS A PSYCHOLOGIST, I work with many parents whose initial goal is to change some aspect of their children's behavior, such as whining, tantrums, aggressiveness, or willfulness. It's tempting to look at what our children do wrong and see the solution as fixing them, but that approach ignores a key principle of change in relationships.

As I said in the introduction, I like to think of relationships as a dance. If one person changes her steps in the dance, the other person must also change his. This is especially true with our children.

So remember that you are the instrument of change in your relationship with your children (or anyone else). If you want someone else to change, start by changing yourself.

For example, we may often feel that our kids don't listen to us. It seems that we have to constantly repeat ourselves and sometimes resort to yelling to get their attention (see also #4). Yelling seems to work, so when we really mean it, this becomes our go-to strategy. We might think to ourselves, "Well, I wouldn't have to yell if they would listen to me." But this perspective overlooks the role we ourselves are playing in this dynamic.

Consider that we may be unintentionally teaching our kids to ignore us until we yell. How? By asking again and again, we send our kids the message that we can be ignored until either we give up ("She didn't really mean it") or we yell ("Now she means it"). In this case, the answer is to stop repeating ourselves. (What to do instead? See #29, 47, 50, and 73 for more tips on how to get kids to listen the first time.)

TRY THIS: Call to mind some aspect of your children's behavior that you wish were different. Now shift the focus to your role and ask yourself: How am I contributing to this situation/behavior/response?

Are you wishing they would stop interrupting you? Ask yourself: Do I stop what I'm doing to focus on their issue when they interrupt? (That is, does their interrupting work?) (See also #23.)

Are you wishing they would stop testing you or breaking rules? Ask yourself: Am I consistent in setting and maintaining limits? (See also #53.)

Are you wishing they would stop whining or yelling? Ask yourself: Do I continue the conversation when they whine or yell? If so, your behavior sends the implicit message that whining or arguing is an acceptable form of communication. (See also #21 and #41.)

Once you've identified your part in the problematic behavior, focus your effort and attention on changing how *you* interact with your kids around this issue. If you are consistent, calm, and firm (but not forceful; see #39 and #54) in maintaining your new response, your kids' behavior will change, too.

Great parents

focus near and far

WHEN WE ARE trying to get dinner on the table and our three-year-old is yelling from the other room that he wants us to help him with something *right now*, it can be easy to focus on the moment at hand (the near) and overlook the big picture (the far). In the moment, it seems to make sense to go help him so that he'll stop yelling and we can finish preparing dinner in peace.

Similarly, when our ten-year-old ambles into the room where we are busy doing something and says with a big sigh, "I'm bored," it seems expedient to rattle off a list of possible activities that might interest her. Or when our children are ignoring us, it may seem like the only way to get their attention is to yell.

In these moments—in the typical day-to-day rush of family life—it's important to pay attention to the long-term implications of our daily interactions with our kids. If, for example, we habitually interrupt our activities when our children demand our attention, then as those moments accumulate over time, we are inadvertently teaching kids that their needs and demands take priority, and we are also not allowing them to practice waiting. (See also #33.)

If we habitually try to "fix" our children's feelings, including boredom, then we are teaching them that some feelings are bad (because they need to be fixed). We are also not allowing our kids the opportunity to learn how to accept and tolerate those feelings when they inevitably come, or how to manage and influence their feelings. (See also #11, 13, and 32.)

Similarly, if we habitually yell to get our kids' attention, we are inadvertently teaching them to ignore us until we yell, and we are also teaching them from our own example that yelling is an acceptable way to get someone's attention. The key word in each of these examples is "habitual"—the grain of rice only becomes a mountain if you keep adding more.

Focusing near and far means that we keep in mind our big-picture goals for our family and children, even as we manage the everyday challenges of family life. It means we don't sacrifice our long-term goals for the sake of a short-term resolution. (See also #34.)

TRY THIS: Pay attention to the things you habitually do and say (or don't do and say). Watch yourself as if you were an outside observer.

Ask yourself these questions about your habitual behaviors:

1. Is what I'm doing something I would be happy to see my kids emulate?
2. Is what I'm doing creating a positive family dynamic?
3. Is what I'm doing solving one problem but creating another?

For example, imagine you are out shopping with your four-year-old and he asks if he can buy a little toy car that caught his eye. You might say, "No, honey, you don't need another car, you already have dozens at home." (But see #6 and #65 for other ways to communicate this that are less likely to provoke frustration.) You try to ignore the loud whining that ensues, but as you continue down the aisles it really starts to bother you, so you decide to relent and get the toy in order to get him to quiet down. After all, three dollars is a small price to pay for a little peace and quiet, right? Maybe not.

Although buying the toy has solved one problem (now he'll stop whining and you can finish shopping in peace), it has likely created another: Your son has just learned that whining works (at least sometimes). This means that the next time he wants to change your mind or get your attention, he's likely to whine again. Your response has reinforced his whining. So you got him to be quiet at the store, but you set yourself up for more whining in the future. (See also #21 and #53.)

If you answer no to questions 1 or 2, or yes to question 3, then seek feedback and support from a trusted friend, family member, or professional to learn and practice new ways of responding to the situations that you have identified as problematic.

5

Great parents

see parenting as a skill

DESPITE THE FACT that raising children is one of the most important endeavors we undertake as humans, there is no training required of us to help us do it to the best of our ability. Every other occupation, even those that don't affect other people's emotional well-being, typically requires some time spent learning and practicing those new skills.

Like almost everything else we do in life, parenting is a skill, and there is a wide body of research that can help us do it more skillfully—with greater confidence, less stress, and better results.

Seeing parenting as a skill also helps us to refrain from judging ourselves harshly when we make mistakes, to maintain an attitude of openness and learning, and to continually seek new and useful information in our effort to keep building our skills.

TRY THIS: Identify your parenting challenges (your kids will help with this!) and seek out new information and tools to build your skills (see also #2).

When you make mistakes, refrain from judging yourself ("I'm a bad mom/dad") and reframe your mistakes as indicating an area in which you need more knowledge, support, and practice.

6

Great parents
practice empathy

EMPATHY MAY BE the single most powerful tool that all parents have, and it's always available. If you don't know what else to do, try empathy. The power of empathy is the power to make someone else feel understood, and that feeling can diffuse any number of otherwise unpleasant situations and power struggles.*

Empathy positively harnesses the power of our emotions, which can easily overtake our reasoning. This is why empathy often works when reasoning fails. (See also #49.)

When we practice empathy with our kids, we show respect for their feelings and their reality (which are often different from ours; see #8). It shows that we are really listening and that we understand (or at least are trying to understand) their point of view.

---

* Strictly speaking, empathy means actually feeling what another person is feeling, in contrast with sympathy, which refers to understanding and caring about another's feelings, without necessarily experiencing those feelings. Parents experience both empathy and sympathy with their children. In order to avoid distracting technical details or terminology, I will use the term "empathy" throughout the book more loosely, to mean focusing on feelings in a way that shows sincerity and respect for another person's way of experiencing the world.

Empathy has the power to sidestep or diffuse power struggles (see #61). Empathy also creates a safe place, emotionally, for our kids to experience hard feelings, like rejection or disappointment.

Please note that practicing empathy does *not* oblige you to change or fix anything about the situation. This is an important distinction. For example, you can offer empathy for your son's frustration at having to wear a seat belt that he finds uncomfortable, without the need to take the seat belt off. You are simply reflecting the feelings you are noticing with genuine understanding, and validating them. (See also #32.)

TRY THIS: The next time you are presented with a parenting challenge of any kind, start with empathy and focus on feelings. It really works (with adults, too).

For instance, your child is getting upset because he has to finish his chores before he can go to a friend's house. Instead of responding by reminding him of why this is so (that is, instead of reasoning with him), begin your response by reflecting his feelings with sincere empathy. We all know what it's like not to have things go our way.

"I know you're upset about having to wait to go to Tim's house. I can see why you would feel frustrated (acknowledge feelings). *I don't like it either when I have to wait to do something I'm looking forward to* (validate feelings)."

Note that expressing empathy will have the most impact when you demonstrate a deep understanding of your child's experience, so statements like "I get it" or "I understand you're upset," while a move in the right direction, will not be as powerful as really showing that you get it.

For example: *"I can see why you'd be angry and disappointed. I told you yesterday that we would go swimming after school today and then I picked you up too late to go. You were looking forward to swimming all day and then it didn't happen."*

In addition to showing empathy for your kids' unique way of experiencing the world, practicing empathy also means that you help kids learn how to imagine other people's perspectives and feelings. This is an essential life skill for maintaining good relationships, which are a cornerstone of happiness and success.

You can do this by asking kids questions like *"How do you think _____ felt when that happened / you did that?"* and also by talking about your feelings in a reflective way (e.g., *"When you don't help clean up after dinner without being reminded, I feel frustrated because it seems that the time I spend cooking isn't appreciated."*)

7

Great parents
watch out for "buts"

PRACTICING EMPATHY (SEE #6) is one of the best ways to strengthen our emotional connection and relationship with our kids. But our good efforts to pause and acknowledge what our child is feeling can be undermined with one small word: "but."

Let me illustrate what I mean, using the example from #6: *"Honey, I know you're upset about having to wait to go to Tim's house. I can see why you would feel frustrated. I don't like it either when I have to wait to do something I'm looking forward to."*

So far, so good. But then we often add this: *"But you know you have to finish your chores before going out."*

"But" is a negating word. When it follows an expression of empathy (as in, "I can see you're upset, *but . . .*") it has the effect of minimizing what came before. This little word can undermine the emotional connection you just created, and reignite conflict.

———

TRY THIS: Instead of saying "but" when you respond to your child's perspective or expression of feelings, try replacing it with the phrase "at the same time." (Other good options are "and" or "also.") Saying "at the same time" implies that both ways of viewing the situation are valid, and this minimizes conflict about which perspective is "better" or "right."

"Honey, I know you're upset about having to wait to go to Tim's house. I don't like it either when I have to wait to do something I'm looking forward to. At the same time, please remember our family rule about finishing chores before going out for the evening."

Same message, less conflict. (See also #65 for another simple wording change that can have a big impact.)

8

Great parents

respect their children's reality

It sounds easy to respect your children's reality—until you discover that it's different from your own. Respecting our children's reality means letting them feel, think, and experience things in a different way than we do. A primary tool for doing this is empathy (#6).

Like over-functioning (#13), not respecting our children's reality is something we are generally unaware of doing. We really have to pay attention (#17) to notice the ways in which we unintentionally disregard or question their feelings and perspective.

Here's a scene I overheard a few years ago, which illustrates a minor example of not respecting our children's reality. A father came to pick up his daughter after a day of camp. She was happily playing with her friends when he arrived. When he told her it was time to go, she replied: "I don't want to go yet. I'm having fun." Her father responded: "But you've been here all day. You've had enough." She started to become upset and protested again that she wasn't ready to go. This exchange went back and forth until eventually the father sternly took his daughter's arm and walked her to the car.

A more skillful way to handle that situation would have been to practice empathy right from the start. When the daughter said she didn't want to go, the father might have responded: *"Sweetie, I can see you're having a lot of fun and you really don't want to go yet* (empathy). *I'm sorry about that. At the same time, we are meeting Mom for dinner and it wouldn't be nice manners to be late* (reason; see #46). *Please say good-bye to your friends and go get your things* (request)."

Here's a second example of how we unintentionally fail to respect our children's reality and how doing so can create conflict when our goal is just the opposite.

A first-grader doing his math homework is struggling. He gets frustrated and says, "I can't do this." Many well-meaning parents respond with something like this: "Yes, you can, sweetie. Here, let me show you."

By telling him that he really can do the problem he is struggling with, you are intending to motivate him to keep trying. Although your intentions are good, you are essentially telling him he is wrong about his experience; you are arguing with his reality.

Paradoxically, this type of response makes some kids even more likely to hold on to their belief that they cannot do it: *"No, I can't!"* Now the situation has unfortunately escalated from frustration with homework to frustration/anger/sadness at not being understood.

A more skillful way to respond in this instance would

be, again, to start with empathy. *"Honey, I can see you're struggling with this and it feels really hard right now* (empathy). *How about a hug* (hug or other positive touch; see #19)? *Okay, show me where you're feeling stuck with this; let's see if we can come up with some other ways of approaching this problem* (coaching; see #45). *I can see this math is tricky for you right now* (avoiding labels; see #43). *At the same time, I believe that you can figure it out."*

In this example, note the important, but subtle, distinction in saying "I believe you can do it" instead of "You can do it." In the first, you are stating your opinion; in the second, you are stating something as a fact that argues with your child's experience.

TRY THIS: Be watchful for opportunities to reflect and show empathy for the different ways in which your child experiences the world. Let your kids have their feelings and perspective, even if you don't understand or agree with them.

If you want to voice your disagreement, try doing so in a way that also acknowledges the validity of their way of seeing things, instead of stating it as a fact. Compare these two hypothetical responses to a child's statement, "This park is no fun. I don't like it."

- Yes, it is. This park is really fun; it's just like the park we usually go to.
- Well, you don't think this park is fun, while I see it

differently. I guess different people like different things.

The second response allows for a difference of opinion, while the first one suggests there is only one right answer (yours).

Similarly, if your child is upset about something, respecting her reality would mean that instead of saying "Don't cry" or "Everything's fine" (both of which don't acknowledge her experience at the moment) you might say, "You're feeling upset right now."

9

Great parents

accept their kids just as they are

Accepting our kids as they are is not the same as loving them. Many parents who love their kids may also shame or reject them for liking, wanting, or thinking things that the parents find intolerable.

As I use the term, "acceptance" includes love, but it is even more difficult than love. You might call it unconditional love.

Accepting your child as he is does not mean, however, that you like or approve of his *behavior*. This is a critical difference. When you accept your child, you love and accept him as he is, although not necessarily what he does. You make a distinction between the child as an individual and his behavior (see #11). (I use the term "behavior" to apply to any action that others can experience, including speech. In this usage, behavior consists of what we do and what we say.)

This distinction between the person and his behavior paves the way for clarity about what is sacred and what is not. Your child's self—his thoughts and feelings—are sacred and your goal should be to understand and accept them. Trying to change your child's thoughts or feelings is unlikely to succeed and will most likely impair your relationship with him (see #39).

On the other hand, your child's behavior, including what he says and does while in your care, are subject to rules about what is okay and what is not.

The bottom line? Behavior is the subject of discipline, while thoughts and feelings are not. (See also #11.)

TRY THIS: Make a distinction between your child's thoughts/feelings and his behavior/speech. For example, if your son tells you in private that he wishes his little brother had never been born, you might be tempted to chastise him for his apparent lack of brotherly love. But your disapproval would not change his feelings, though it might make it more likely that your son avoids sharing his feelings with you in the future.

Instead, let him have his feelings, and try to be curious about them. *"Honey, why do you feel that way?"* (His answer might also help you to identify ways to help him grow to love his brother.) Feel free to share your feelings about what you are hearing (see #15), as long as you can do so without shaming or guilt-tripping him (see #10). *"I didn't know you felt that way. I'm glad you told me. Still, I feel sad to hear it."*

At the same time, if at any point you observe your son *behave* toward his younger brother in a way that is unacceptable, then by all means set clear rules and boundaries. But until your child's feelings turn into action, they are only feelings. (See also #19.)

10

Great parents

avoid these toxic phrases

Have you ever heard yourself say any of the following?

- *"You're making me crazy!"*
- *"What's wrong with you!"*
- *"You are a bad boy/girl!"*
- *"You'd better _____ or else!"*

In the momentum of the present—trying to get kids out the door to school or to get dinner on the table—we often find ourselves saying or doing things without considering the long-term impact of our words or actions (see also #4).

While it can be incredibly difficult to choose our words carefully in the heat of the moment, our words can have a significant impact on our kids, especially when they are repeated regularly. If those words are frequently harsh or blaming, odds are our relationship with our kids will suffer.

Instead, great parents strive to communicate with both their words and actions that they love their kids no matter what—even when they disapprove of their child's behavior (i.e., what kids say or what they do).

I call this principle "separating kids from their behavior" (see #9). In so doing, we can maintain a strong emotional connection with our kids (#39) even when we discipline their behavior. This principle also reinforces the related ideas that behavior is a choice (#11) and that kids are works in progress (#36).

The problem with the earlier toxic phrases is that they use blame ("You're making me crazy"), shame ("What's wrong with you?" or "You are a bad boy/girl!"), and fear ("You'd better _____ or else!") to motivate behavior change, rather than an authoritative (#38) and matter-of-fact (#54) approach based on reasons (#46), empathy (#6), and rehearsals (#73). They focus attention on the child as a whole, instead of on his behavior.

In almost every situation, the problem at hand is what the child said and/or did (what I refer to as behavior). Using blame, shame, or fear will eventually backfire because these strategies don't focus on the real problem (behavior) and imply instead that the child himself is the problem. This is a recipe for impaired well-being.

Using words that convey blame ("You're making me crazy!") frames the situation as being your child's fault, rather than acknowledging that all situations are a complex product of many different inputs, including our own perceptions, moods, prior experiences, and expectations.

Phrases that use shame ("What's wrong with you?") suggest to kids that they are flawed and focus their attention on what's wrong with them as a person, rather than on what they can do differently in the future to help create a more positive outcome.

In the case of the fear-inducing phrase ("You'd better _____ or else"), the underlying message to kids is that aggression and intimidation are an acceptable way to get what they want (i.e., if you're doing it, why shouldn't they?).

Remember, too, that much of what looks like misbehavior is experimentation (see #34) or a misguided attempt to meet a perceived need (see #21).

Instead, we can teach children that behavior is a choice and emphasize that they can learn to make better choices. Making a bad choice or misbehaving does not mean they are bad people, only that they made a mistake and need more practice and coaching (see #45 and #73) to do better next time.

TRY THIS: Try one of these alternative phrases to keep the focus on your child's behavior. Be sure to pair these phrases with a brief explanation of *why* the behavior is problematic, and then discuss (and maybe also rehearse) what your child could do differently next time.

- *"I don't like that behavior."*
- *"I don't like it when you _____ because _____."*
- *"It's not okay for you to _____ because _____."*

For example, if you walk into the living room and find that your six-year-old has just cut your favorite sofa pillow into shreds, you might be tempted to exclaim, "What's wrong with you?" Instead, remember that your child's behavior is almost always an attempt to meet a perceived need, such as getting your attention, getting information (What happens if I do this?), or creative engagement (This would be fun to do).

Pause, take a deep breath, and say something like this, which keeps the focus on behavior instead of personality: *"It's not okay for you to damage something that doesn't belong to you. I am really mad that you did that* (own feelings, #15). *I know it's fun to use the scissors* (empathy). *At the same time, those pillows are mine and now they can't be fixed* (reason). *Why did you cut the pillows* (understand goal or perceived need)?*"

Once you understand their goal, you can suggest alternative methods (see #22) for next time, and if appropriate, give fair warning of consequences (see #47).

Final note: In addition to using your words to keep the focus on your child's behavior, pay attention also to your nonverbal communication—body language, tone of voice, gestures, etc. These nonverbal cues are powerful and can shift the meaning of your words. (See #30.)

11

Great parents

teach kids to feel their feelings
and choose their actions

FEELINGS ARE WHAT they are. Try as we may, we generally cannot change or control them at will. (Consider how often you are able to successfully "snap out of it" when someone else suggests it.) We can, however, acknowledge and accept our feelings, and know that they will change, since that is the nature of feelings. (We can also help them change; see #32.)

Behavior, on the other hand, is much more within our power to control.

Behavior, ultimately, is a *choice*, although it can be tempting to excuse our bad behavior by blaming our feelings ("I was just so mad") or by blaming others ("You made me so mad!").

Even though we may be in the throes of a strong emotion, such as anger, we always have the opportunity to pause and make a choice about how we want to *respond* to the situation. We don't have to *say* what we are thinking or *act* on our feelings.

Our feelings may be compelling us, for example, to yell or be sarcastic, but we can choose not to follow our feelings into action. Instead, we can make a choice to respond as constructively and skillfully as we can.

However, once we are already feeling a strong emotion, our ability to think creatively about better and more skillful responses tends to be impaired (see #49). For this reason, it's helpful to consider, plan, and even practice alternative responses in advance, when we are calm and relaxed. (See also #73.)

Great parents coach their kids in how to feel their feelings and choose their actions, which is to say, how to respond instead of react. Great parents also model this principle themselves. Through instruction and by example, let your kids know that it's okay to feel whatever they're feeling, but it may not be okay (or constructive) to follow those feelings into action (by yelling, hitting, avoiding, etc.).

For specific guidance on how to teach kids this principle, see emotion coaching (#32).

TRY THIS: Here's a sample scenario to illustrate this practice. Imagine your daughter has just come home past her curfew. You had already given her fair warning (see #47) that the consequence for breaking curfew would be not going out the following weekend, which in this case would mean missing her best friend's slumber party. Frustrated, she lashes out at you: "I hate you! You're a terrible mom!"

The conflict is likely to escalate if you hit, yell back

("How dare you!"), or react ("You have only yourself to blame"). Instead, staying matter-of-fact (see #54), you might say: *"Honey, I can see that you're really upset and wish this hadn't happened, and if it were me, I would also feel disappointed about missing Debbie's party* (empathy; see #6).

"It's okay for you to be angry with me, even to feel that you hate me right now (validate feelings). *At the same time, it's not okay for you to say those words out loud to me* (choose your actions). *It's okay to think it and feel it, but saying it out loud is disrespectful and hurtful* (reason). *Let's discuss this in the morning when we can both be calmer* (stop the action, #71)." Now disengage.

If your child keeps trying to pull you back into the conversation ("You never listen!" "You don't care!" etc.), matter-of-factly repeat your statement that you will discuss it later when everyone is calm. Don't get provoked into reentering the conversation, and keep repeating your statement, *"We'll discuss this tomorrow morning when everyone is calm."*

12

Great parents
aren't perfect

ALL PARENTS MAKE mistakes. This is part of the learning process and also part of being human. I have yet to meet a parent, including myself, who doesn't make mistakes.

Even after we develop our skills as a parent (see #5), mistakes still happen for two main reasons:

1. We aren't paying attention (see #17). For example, we are distracted and don't notice that our anger has been growing and is on the verge of exploding. Then we find ourselves yelling. Or we don't notice that our child is whining when she asks us for something, and we reflexively give it to her (see #23).
2. We aren't doing what we know (see #2). For example, we know we should be consistent (#53), but we are just too tired to follow through.

Great parents take responsibility for their mistakes and know that apologizing to their children when it's called for is a powerful way to teach integrity and to model what to do when you make a mistake. However, if you find yourself repeatedly apologizing for the same thing(s), the effect of your apology will be diminished over time. In this case, consider seeking support from a mental health professional to help you understand and change any ongoing, problematic behavior.

Great parents know that an apology does not undermine their authority as parents, but rather, it demonstrates confidence, integrity, and responsibility.

It's also important to keep in mind that, in most cases, making minor mistakes in your parenting life will have little effect on how your children turn out as adults. Research shows that parents have only a partial influence on their children's adult personality and behavior.[1]

Being able to take responsibility for our mistakes requires us to develop our self-awareness (#18) and to take ownership of our own feelings and moods (#15). You will be pleasantly surprised when your kids start to do the same.

TRY THIS: The next time you find yourself having done something that does not fit with your values or standards (e.g., losing your patience and yelling at your kids), give yourself time to calm down and then say something like this: *"I'm sorry that I yelled at you earlier today. I had a challenging day at work and I was low on patience. Still, yelling at you was not okay and I'm very sorry."*

13

Great parents
let kids make mistakes and
experience failure

BE YOUR CHILDREN'S coach in life. Let them be the players.

What I call "over-functioning" as a parent can take many different forms—finishing your kid's homework, bringing your five-year-old's coat to school after she left it at home (again), accepting your toddler's garbage as he hands it to you before running off to play after snack time—but the common denominator is doing something for your children that they can do, or can learn to do, for themselves.

For example, if you always bring your child's coat (or lunch, homework, or whatever) to school after she forgets it at home, she won't have the unpleasant experience—of *not* having a coat (or lunch or homework)—that will in turn motivate her to do it for herself.

If you always remind your child to do her homework so she won't forget and receive a poor mark in school, again you are doing something for her that in the short term may be helpful, but in the long term is problematic because your child is not getting the opportunity to learn how to be responsible for herself or to practice important life skills such as time management. (See also #4 and #45)

Parents often over-function without even realizing it. They do this partly because life is busy and they are just trying to get through the daily tasks, partly because they can do things better and faster than their kids, and partly because they prefer not to see their kids be uncomfortable or not to do well.

However, making mistakes and experiencing "failure," disappointment, and discomfort are essential life experiences that provide the opportunity for kids to learn how to do better and to practice new skills. It's natural for parents to want to buffer kids from these unpleasant experiences, but we make an enormous future trade-off when we do so.

We may be averting some short-term pain or discomfort (both for us and them), but in the long run, we may also be inadvertently depriving our children of the opportunity to learn and practice important life skills while they are still in the supportive environment of our family.

Here's another big downside of over-functioning: It can also become a source of power struggles. Take the previous example of reminding your kids to do their homework. It often happens that, as you remind (and eventually insist) that they do their homework, they procrastinate and resist, and then a power struggle develops. What would happen if you didn't start down that path at all?

Please note that I am not advocating a scenario in which you never help your kids out, or never do something for them that they can do themselves. Helping each other out and pitching in are important values in a family. My point here is just to think about what you do regularly for your kids and determine whether they could benefit from learning to do it themselves. Confidence and true self-esteem are both derived from the sense of competence that comes from learning new skills, mistakes and all.

TRY THIS: Pay attention to the many things you do for your children and ask yourself:

- Why am I doing this?
- Are my children capable of doing this for themselves or, in the case of household chores, for the family? (If so, consider teaching them.)
- What would happen if I didn't do this for them?

Experiment with not doing some of the things you typically do, and let them know in advance that they should not expect that from you anymore.

"I've noticed that I tend to remind you every night about your homework (self-awareness, #18). *I think you can remember to do your homework on your own* (benefit of the doubt, #36), *so I'm going to stop reminding you* (fair warning, #47). *If you forget, or choose not to do it, that's up to you*

(autonomy), *though if that happens regularly, I think it's going to affect your grades* (preview of natural consequences; see #35 and #50). *If you ever want help with your homework, I'm always happy to support you, so just ask."*

What if your children need help remembering or organizing their time? (See #45.)

It can be scary to stop ourselves from doing many of the things we parents do to ease our children's lives and protect them from adverse consequences—such as reminding them to do homework—but if we don't stop now, it gets increasingly harder as kids get older and are still relying on us to do those things.

Here's another (minor) example of over-functioning: A child who has just finished a snack or other activity comes over to Mom or Dad, hands over the garbage, and runs off to play. Mom or Dad takes the garbage and throws it away. If you have ever done this, why did you? If your children can walk, they can take their own garbage to the receptacle. This is a good habit for them to learn.

Great parents

resist the urge to "fix" feelings

LIKE THE URGE to "fix" situations (such as forgetting homework or lunch), the urge to "fix" feelings comes from a similar place of good intentions: the desire to spare our children from discomfort, disappointment, and failure (e.g., being cold, being hungry, being chastised by the teacher, getting poor grades, and so on). Fixing feelings is actually just a more subtle example of over-functioning (see #13).

In the case of fixing feelings, we are trying to spare our children from experiencing unpleasant or painful emotions, ranging from something relatively minor like boredom to something more significant like social rejection. In most cases, we are also trying to spare *ourselves* from the distress of seeing our children experience unpleasant or painful feelings (see #15). It's no easy task, but we must learn how to tolerate our children's discomfort, so that they can, too. I'll repeat that since it's such an important principle: Learn to tolerate your child's discomfort, so she can, too.

Although it is understandable for parents to want to

buffer children (and themselves) from these experiences, in so doing, parents inadvertently deprive children of the opportunity to learn and practice good coping skills, with their help and guidance.

Here are two examples illustrating what I mean by "fixing feelings":

1. Your child comes into the room where you are working, sighs, and declares, "I'm bored." It's easy to reflexively respond to this complaint with a long list of potential activities. But this response encourages kids to look to you in the future to solve this "problem" instead of grappling with it themselves.

Instead, consider allowing your child to experience boredom. Why? People are inclined to avoid unpleasant experiences, so if boredom is unpleasant for your kids, they are likely to come up with their own solutions. Now they will have engaged their imaginations and also learned that they can resolve challenges.

If you feel you must help them solve their boredom "problem" (or a similar situation), resist the temptation to tell them exactly what to do in favor of talking them through how to solve their problem. Narrate the process. For example: "Well, what are some things you have enjoyed doing in the past? Let's make a list." (See also #45.)

2. When you pick your child up from school, she says tearfully, "Everyone hates me." This is a very painful thing to hear as a parent, so a common and natural re-

sponse to this is, "No, they don't, honey! What about Amanda? She's your friend." It's probably true that your child's perception of the situation is not entirely accurate, but telling her this, even nicely, may make her feel unheard and misunderstood (see also #8).

Trying to fix her feelings may also communicate the idea that those feelings are "bad" (instead of an emotional experience that is normal and will pass) or that your child can't handle those feelings (so you have to step in). Also, as I noted earlier, trying to fix feelings doesn't give our children the chance to learn how to tolerate those feelings or to practice emotion regulation skills to manage them.

TRY THIS: When you notice that your child is experiencing a feeling that you have the urge to fix (e.g., boredom, rejection, anxiety), pause and remind yourself that this is an opportunity for your child to practice some useful life skills with your guidance.

Start by empathizing with her feelings (see #6): "Oh, honey, I'll bet you feel really sad and lonely when you think that everyone hates you. That would feel really terrible to me, too." See where this conversation starter takes you.

When the time feels right, you can step into the role of coach, using open-ended questions to elicit your child's perspective and encouraging her to try on alternative viewpoints: "So, what happened today that makes you think everyone hates you? . . . Oh, so the other girls *seemed to ignore you when you wanted to play with them?* (reflection) . . . *Are there any other explanations that might also explain what happened?"* And so on.

Part of the goal here is to help your child look at the situation from other perspectives, and hopefully conclude (in most cases) that there are other, equally valid ways of interpreting what happened.

Remember that you don't have to fix the situation or make your child feel better. Just offer your compassion and presence. Help your child learn to feel her feelings and to choose her actions (see #11 and #32).

If the situation calls for a response of some kind, support your child by discussing her options with her and walking her through (but not dictating to her) the process for making a choice about how to respond. (There are, of course, situations in which adults should step in immediately, such as bullying or abuse.)

15

Great parents

take ownership of their feelings

WE ARE EACH responsible for our own feelings and actions, even though it's common to think that we wouldn't be *feeling* something if someone else hadn't *done* (or not done) something.

It often seems, especially in the heat of the moment, that our kids have "made" us angry and therefore it's "their" fault. However, our feelings are based on a complex web of beliefs, expectations, genetics, experience, and habits, and these have more to do with who *we* are than what anyone else has done *to* us.

For example, imagine a scenario in which our child is sitting across the room playing and we tell him to stop and please come to dinner, but he doesn't respond. If we believe that he isn't listening to us because he is willfully ignoring us, then we are likely to feel angry and react accordingly. If, on the other hand, we believe that he isn't listening to us because he is absorbed in what he is doing (see #29) or because he is testing us to see what will happen if he ignores us (see #34), then we are more likely to remain calm and find another way to get his attention. To put it simply, how we *respond* depends on how we *perceive*.

It's also worth noting that we may have inadvertently contributed to our children's habit of not listening because we often repeat ourselves over and over. For what to do instead, see #46, 47, 51, 71, and 72.

Being responsible for our own feelings does not mean that whatever your kids have done (i.e., their behavior) is okay, and you may still need to deal with that. It only means that your kids are not responsible for how *you* feel about what *they* did. They are only responsible for *their* feelings and *their* actions.

TRY THIS: The next time you find yourself feeling angry or frustrated with your kids, ask yourself: *Why am I feeling this?* (See also #18.)

Question the belief underlying the explanation you give yourself. How do you know it's true?

Remember that your thoughts are just that: They are your thoughts, and not necessarily the truth about the situation. They are your interpretation about what is happening, not the happening itself.

In addition, you will get a lot less pushback if you take responsibility for your feelings (by saying, for example, "I'm annoyed" instead of "You're annoying"). The latter is likely to provoke defensiveness in the other person and escalate the conflict, while the first is harder to argue with since it's simply a statement of how you feel.

Regardless of how you are feeling, remember that you will be most effective in any situation if, instead of reacting, you pause and make a choice about how to respond constructively based on your goals (see #11 and #32).

See also #16.

16

Great parents

acknowledge their moods and feelings

WHEN WE GET home after a stressful day at work, that stress and the feelings that go along with it often carry over into our demeanor when we are reunited with our family. Our kids, who are astute students of our moods and behaviors (see #34), will almost certainly notice our changed demeanor. They may even ask us about it.

Similarly, if we receive some news that profoundly affects us (e.g., the death of a loved one, loss of a job, medical diagnosis, etc.), our kids will notice the change in us, even if we are trying our best to keep it to ourselves.

Many parents, in an effort to spare their children from sharing any unpleasant or painful feelings, will often try to keep those feelings private. They will not talk about what has happened, or how they are feeling, in the hopes that their children won't notice and so won't suffer. This effort, though motivated by love, often backfires, since even very young children are capable of recognizing emotions, discerning stress, and experiencing empathy.[2]

When we are feeling sad, grumpy, or irritated, our

kids and others who know us well can feel it. If we try to hide those feelings ("Everything's fine, honey. Why do you ask?"), we are creating an incongruity between what we say is happening and what our children *feel* is happening (see also #30 and #31).

Kids' empathic "feelers" are picking up on our nonverbal cues (body language, tone of voice, etc.), but we are telling them that their intuitive sense is wrong. This incongruity can be profoundly frightening for children, since they may be strongly feeling that something is wrong, but this feeling is being invalidated by a trusted adult or authority figure. Over time, this recurring invalidation may make it harder for kids to trust their own feelings.

When we hide our feelings, we are also sending the message to kids that some feelings are so bad they have to be hidden. Hiding feelings also inhibits the development of self-awareness (see #18) and emotion regulation skills (see #32), since kids cannot learn to manage feelings they don't know how to recognize.

Instead, parents can model self-awareness and emotional intelligence by taking ownership of their feelings (see #15) and acknowledging those feelings with their kids in an age-appropriate way. So what you might share with your twelve-year-old would be quite different from what you share with your two-year-old.

When you share your own feelings with kids, that's also a good opportunity to share with them the strategies that you use to manage those feelings.

TRY THIS: The next time you come home in a bad/sad/mad mood, don't wait for your kids to ask you about it. They have probably noticed but aren't saying anything. But if they do ask you about it, be sure to acknowledge your feelings, even if you don't give many details about the situation giving rise to them.

Here's an example of what you might say to a two-year-old: *"Mommy is feeling mad and sad right now because of something that happened at work today. Someone was mean to me today and I'm still upset about it. So if I seem a little cranky to you right now, that's why."*

For a twelve-year-old: *"Honey, I'm probably going to be very distracted and irritable tonight, so please give me some space. I felt unfairly criticized by my boss today and I'm frustrated about what happened. I'm also trying to decide what to do about it."*

This kind of feeling talk is invaluable to kids. In addition to modeling self-awareness and emotional intelligence skills, it also teaches kids about the influence of mental states on their own and others' behavior (often called "mentalization"). The ability to mentalize enables children to understand that people's thoughts and feelings impact how they act in the world, and this understanding is critical to developing the ability to "feel your feelings and choose your actions" (#11).

17

Great parents
pay attention

PAYING ATTENTION TO what is actually happening in the here and now can be surprisingly difficult. As adults, we are so often thinking about the past (Did I say the right thing to my boss?) or planning for the future (Remember to pick up eggs on the way home) that it's easy to miss what is happening right in front of us, and even right inside us. Our urge to multitask, plus distracting devices like smartphones, can make paying attention to the here and now even more challenging.

Like self-awareness (#18), paying attention to ourselves, the moment, and others with us in this moment is a cornerstone of great parenting (and of life itself). When we aren't paying attention to ourselves, we can miss cues, such as a racing heartbeat or loud voice, that would alert us to our growing anger before it escalates beyond our control.

When we aren't paying attention to the moment, we may miss the fact that we just handed our whining child the toy she wanted in order to buy ourselves some quiet time (see #23). When we aren't paying attention to our child, we may not notice that he is speaking to us disrespectfully, but we are continuing the conversation anyway, intent on getting our point across.

Many of us operate on autopilot much of the time, not noticing or thinking much about the effects of our moment-to-moment feelings and interactions (see also #4). But if we don't notice what is happening, we can do little to change it (see also #2 and #12).

TRY THIS: The simple truth is this: To get better at paying attention we must practice paying attention. Meditation is one way to do this, and abundant research has shown that a regular meditation practice has innumerable physical and mental health benefits. One excellent source for meditation instruction is the UCLA Mindful Awareness Research Center. For more resources, visit www.DrEricaR.com.

If a formal meditation practice is unappealing to you, you can achieve many of the same benefits from stopping regularly throughout your day to pay attention to the here and now: your breathing, the feel of the sun on your skin, the sensation of your body sitting in the chair, the feel of your hands holding this book. If you find it hard to remember to do this, because it's not yet a habit (see #20), you might try setting an alarm every hour or two to remind you.

18

Great parents
cultivate self-awareness

SELF-AWARENESS IS A cornerstone of great parenting. If we aren't aware of our thoughts and feelings, our emotional triggers, our assumptions, expectations, and so on, then it will be difficult for us to acknowledge our mistakes (#12), respond instead of react (#11), or acknowledge our feelings (#16).

People who have developed self-awareness are reflective about their own perceptions, assumptions, expectations, and beliefs. They work hard to understand how their thoughts and feelings affect their behavior and choices. They also tend to be more empathic and are able to hold different perspectives in mind simultaneously, without one perspective having to be more "right" than the others.

This skill of perspective taking is enormously helpful to parents, who must interact daily with another being who sees the world in a (sometimes very) different way (see #8).

———

TRY THIS: Self-awareness can be cultivated in many different ways. Psychotherapy with a skilled clinician is one way, as are journaling, meditating, and asking for feedback from trusted friends and family.

Spend some time every day paying attention to your thoughts and feelings, noticing how they are interrelated and how together they influence your behavior. For example, if your child is not responding to you when you are calling to him, notice what is happening in your mind and body.

If your thought is "He's ignoring me," then you are more likely to feel frustrated, and thus more likely to yell or be annoyed. In contrast, if your thought is "He's so focused on what he's doing he doesn't even hear me" (see #29), then you are more likely to feel patient, and thus more likely to walk over to him and get his attention.

Even if your thought is "He's ignoring me to see how I'll respond" (see #34), this small change in your interpretation can help you to approach the situation with greater calm and compassion.

19

Great parents
practice positive touch

RESEARCH CONSISTENTLY SHOWS that positive touch (e.g., hugs, caresses, cuddles) is absolutely critical to children's development and ongoing well-being. So critical, in fact, that infants deprived of touch often suffer delays in physical and cognitive development, and can even die. This can happen even if they are regularly fed and all their other physical needs are met.[3] Touch is life.

For people of any age, positive touch promotes health, relaxation, and bonding—oxytocin (the "love hormone") levels increase, heart rate decreases, stress hormones decrease, and immune system functioning is boosted. The bottom line? Hug your kids (a lot).

Even when you discipline your child, aim to end the episode with a hug or other positive touch, especially for younger children. This loving gesture emphasizes that although you are disciplining poor behavior, you are still maintaining an emotional connection with your child (see also #9 and #25). Positive touch also reinforces the effects of praise (see #42 and #73).

On a related note, do not spank or be physically aggressive with kids. Spanking and other forms of physical discipline may appear to work in the moment, but in the long term they teach children to use aggression and violence to resolve conflict or to get what they want.[4] They are also associated with impaired mental health, such as depression and anxiety, as well as reduced cognitive abilities. Instead of physical discipline like spanking, try the practices in this book, such as #6, 46, and 47.

It's important to note that giving children a hug after being aggressive or violent with them is not an antidote to aggression.[5] It does not work to be warm and affectionate following physical aggression in an attempt to make up for it. Instead, parents must strive to maintain a warm and caring connection with their children even when disapproving of their children's behavior or disciplining them (see #39).

Most of the practices in this book are intended to help you maintain a strong emotional bond with your children even when you disapprove of their behavior or discipline them.

TRY THIS: Take time out every day to give your kids (and other loved ones) a long hug or cuddle. If your child doesn't want to cuddle anymore, try a caress on the arm or a loving pat on the back. Show your love daily with touch as well as words. You will both benefit.

20

Great parents

help kids develop positive habits

FROM BIRTH THROUGH age five are especially critical years for children's development: Neural connections and pathways are being formed at an astonishing pace, with the brain growing to about 90 percent of its final adult size. These neural pathways are like paths in a forest—once they are established they tend to persist and become even more used.

As a psychologist, I think of neural pathways as habits and beliefs—those things we find ourselves doing, thinking, and feeling without really trying. These can be habits of thought (such as pessimism or optimism), habits of feeling (such as gratitude or anxiety), and habits of behavior (such as saying "please" and "thank you" or clearing dishes from the table after eating).

It's very much to our and our children's advantage if those habits are positive ones.

Good habits we can help our children learn and practice range from the simple—such as brushing their teeth every night or using nice manners—to the significant, such as turning to books or outdoor play instead of screens for enjoyment, being able to manage strong feelings (see #32), being resilient (see #42), or being patient, helpful, and optimistic.

Habits develop from frequency and repetition. Anything we do, say, think, or feel regularly can be considered a habit in this sense, so if we want to create or change a habit, then we must practice that new behavior, thought, or feeling repeatedly until it becomes habitual.

The early years are truly formative for our kids and our relationship with them. We can give ourselves and our kids a tremendous head start by practicing the principles in this book, so that the habits and beliefs they develop in their early years are constructive ones that serve them well.[6] As Frederick Douglass is thought to have said: "It is easier to build strong children than to repair broken men."

TRY THIS: Consider your daily interactions with your children. Ask yourself:

- What are they learning from these frequent and repeated interactions?
- What sorts of habits—of thought, feeling, and behavior—do you notice being formed in your children's daily experience?
- Are these useful and constructive habits? If not,

take action now to change them (and start by changing yourself; see #3).

Here's a simple example: If your child often interrupts you, start by noticing when it's happening. Then, when you notice this unwanted behavior, do not stop what you are doing to answer him (unless it's an emergency). This alone can be challenging. Instead, say matter-of-factly and repeat as needed: *"You are interrupting me. Please wait until I'm done talking with Ms. Roberts* (or whatever you are doing)." When you are done, give your child your full attention.

With a small child, for whom waiting can be especially difficult, you might say instead: *"Honey, you're interrupting me. If you need my attention when I'm talking to someone else, please say 'excuse me.'"* Then wait until he says it before giving him your full attention. (See #22.)

This change in *your* behavior will help your child practice the habit of waiting his turn to speak, or at least saying "excuse me" first.

Another example: If you want your child to become someone who reads books for pleasure (a habit that pays a lifetime of dividends), actions you can take to reinforce this habit include: reading to him regularly, making fun trips to the library, limiting screen time and keeping screens on the periphery of family life, reading on your own, talking about books, and so on.

Habits may seem insignificant but they can have an enormous impact on our lives. Instead of grades, trophies, or other external achievements, focus on your children's habits and the values underlying them. To paraphrase a favorite quote of mine: "Watch your actions, they become habits; watch your habits, they become character; watch your character, for it becomes your destiny."

21

Great parents

distinguish between goals and methods

WHEN WE FIND ourselves rushed and trying to get dinner on the table while our three-year-old is whining for a glass of milk, it can be helpful to remind ourselves that our child's behavior (whining) has a worthy goal: to get our attention and get a glass of milk.

If you think of examples from your own parenting experience, you'll find that in most cases, the goal your kids are pursuing is worthy—it's their method that's problematic (in this example, the method is whining).

So make a distinction between goals and methods when you address their behavior. Identify their goal and show them how to achieve it through other, more acceptable methods that are within their capabilities to do.

Note that it's also important to show kids that their (undesirable) method is ineffective, too. If they are able to achieve their goal (milk and/or attention, in the example above) by their chosen method (whining), then they are likely to repeat that method in the future because it worked (see #23). Keep in mind that goals can be tangible, like milk, or intangible, like attention.

Whether it's whining or grabbing or any other behavior you'd like to minimize, this distinction between goals and methods will help you acknowledge and empathize with what your kids want, while still teaching them how to achieve their goals with appropriate behaviors.

TRY THIS: Here's how you might respond in the previous example, using the principle of goals versus methods: *"Sweetie, I can see that you really want some milk* (acknowledgment of goal/empathy, #6), *and when you whine at me it hurts my ears and distracts me from making dinner* (reason, #46).

"If you would like some milk, please say: 'Momma, can I please have some milk?' (alternative method)." As soon as she makes an effort to use the alternative method, give her the milk (or whatever her goal is).

The same principle holds for an older child. Instead of a two-year-old whining for milk while you are making dinner, imagine your teenager wants to borrow your car (goal). When you put her off because you're busy preparing dinner, she starts following you around the kitchen, saying, "Come on, Mom. Please? Please!" and continuing her campaign (method).

In this case, you might say, *"Honey, I can see you are really hoping to borrow the car and want to know right away if you can* (acknowledgment of goal). *At the same time, when you follow me around the kitchen after I've asked you to wait until I'm done preparing dinner, I feel badgered* (reason; ownership of feelings). *If you keep doing that, the answer is definitely no* (fair warning). *If you want to talk about borrowing the car, let's do it when dinner's on the table* (alternative method)."

Read #22 for more tips on how to talk to kids about goals versus methods.

22

Great parents

show kids the way

WHEN WE DISCIPLINE kids, a primary goal is to teach them (see #28) that the behavior in question (e.g., hitting, drawing on the furniture) is unacceptable.

One component of effective discipline is giving fair and reasonable consequences (#51) with fair warning (#47). However, consequences can only suppress behavior—they convey the message that the behavior in question is not okay, but that is only half of the story that kids need to hear.

The other half to tell kids is the kind of behavior that is acceptable. This is what I mean by showing kids the way (aka giving alternatives), and it goes hand in hand with distinguishing between goals and methods (#21).

Many parents overlook this crucial step of giving alternatives. You'll know this is happening when you hear yourself saying "Stop that" or "Please don't _____" without also telling kids what they could do instead.

If parents don't tell kids what kind of behavior they would like to see instead, then kids will often fill that information gap on their own, often with less-than-desirable outcomes. So the next time you find yourself telling your kids that their behavior is not okay, be sure to pair it with a discussion (for older kids) or instruction (for younger kids) of what would be a better alternative (and why).

Then ask for a replay (#72) or stage a rehearsal (#73), and give them a chance to practice this new and improved behavior in response to the situation that evoked the problematic behavior. Be ready to respond positively when they try it (see #23, 24, 42, and 68).

For example:

"I know you really wanted to read two books instead of one tonight and you're feeling upset and frustrated (empathy; see #6). *At the same time, it's not okay for you to throw your books on the floor because books are special and we need to take care of them* (reason; see #46). *Instead, you could say, 'Daddy, I'm disappointed that we can't read two books tonight. Could you please make sure we have time for two books tomorrow night?'* (give alternative)."

There are two important guidelines to keep in mind. The alternative method you specify should be both

1. a more acceptable behavior and
2. something your child can do successfully. This will vary by your child's capabilities and temperament. For example, it's unlikely that a high-energy two-year-old can successfully wait for five minutes to get a glass of milk, but she can say "please" in a polite voice.

Giving alternatives is also a preferable starting point to giving consequences, since it gives kids an opportunity to redirect their own behavior and it gives you an opportunity to reinforce that improved behavior instead of giving a consequence.

TRY THIS: The next time you ask your child to change her behavior, first ask yourself what she might be trying to accomplish and then propose (or discuss) a more acceptable way to achieve that goal. Ask for a replay or stage a rehearsal.

For example, your toddler might be playing with her sippy cup at the table, pouring it out, shaking it, and so on. Recognize that she's engaged in an activity she finds interesting (see #34), but she's doing it at the wrong time and place.

You might say, *"Please don't play with your milk at the table* (request) *because it makes a mess/disrupts dinner/etc.* (reason). *If you want to play with your sippy cup, you can bring it with you in the bathtub tonight/take it outside in the yard* (alternative)."

If she persists, matter-of-factly (#54) take her sippy cup away for a brief moment (not more than a minute) and then give it back to her so she can try again. I call this a "replay." Repeat as needed.

Read #21 for more tips on how to talk to kids about alternative behaviors.

23

Great parents

don't gratify behavior
they don't want repeated

WHEN KIDS BEHAVE in a negative way, they are likely to repeat it if the response or result is close to their desired outcome (see also #21). So if refusing to help clean up the toys in the living room means that Dad will eventually give up insisting and just do it himself (even if only sometimes; see #53), then kids are likely to keep refusing. It worked before, didn't it?

Similarly, I consult with many parents of adolescents who would like their children to speak more politely to them. (First question: What behavior are you modeling for your kids? Do you speak to them respectfully? See #40.)

What these parents often discover when they start paying closer attention (#17) to their family interactions is that they have entire conversations in which their child is yelling at them or otherwise speaking disrespectfully. Throughout these conversations, the parent might say several times, "It's not okay to talk to me like that," but the conversation continues anyway. Parents *say* it's not okay but their behavior tells the opposite story.

More often than not, parents end up yelling back at

their child in this situation, which perpetuates the cycle of yelling. (Yelling at your children to stop yelling will not teach them to stop.)

However, even if parents manage to stay calm when their child is yelling (or whining), if they still continue the interaction they are unintentionally teaching their child that yelling or whining is an acceptable way to communicate. (What to do instead in this situation? A key tool for avoiding this dynamic is stopping the action; see #71.)

TRY THIS: Pay close attention to the interactions that often lead to conflict or frustration with your child. Think about your child's behavior in terms of methods and goals (see #21), and observe your response to your child's problematic behavior. Does your behavior unintentionally reinforce hers?

Does your response help her achieve her goal, either explicitly (as with cleaning up the toys yourself) or implicitly (as with continuing a conversation in which your child is yelling at you)? If so, you will need to change your response in order to change your child's behavior (see also #3).

You can start the process of change by planning (and even rehearsing; see #73) your new response in advance. Other useful tools are stopping the action and, when appropriate, asking for a replay (#72).

24

Great parents

"catch" kids being good (and tell kids
specifically what they liked)

PARENTS OFTEN FOCUS a lot of time and energy pointing out things kids can improve. It's important to balance those messages with acknowledgments of things
kids are already doing well. Like adults, kids want to
feel appreciated.

Kids thrive on enthusiastic, specific, and immediate
feedback. Particularly when you are trying to reshape
challenging behavior, be proactive in watching for your
children's attempts to do better and promptly acknowledge them for it. Even a small step forward is worthy of
acknowledgment (see #45).

In addition to watching for good behavior, parents
can also support kids by creating the conditions for
them to behave well. Be sure kids are well rested and fed
(see #27 and #58), and create structure around their activities to minimize the chance of misbehavior and encourage good behavior (see #52). For example, if your
child has a hard time sharing toys with visiting friends,
encourage her to put away any special toys before her
playmates arrive, so that you don't later have to inter-

vene in a tug-of-war. When you see an instance of good behavior, reinforce it with praise (see below for specific guidelines). (See also #73.)

When we praise our kids, it's important to be specific (see also #42). So instead of just saying "Good job!" think about what exactly you are praising and be specific.

In addition, look for ways to reinforce your praise nonverbally, by including a hug, friendly pat, or other positive touch (#19). For example: *"Dylan, I noticed that you were frustrated that your sister took your toy away without asking, but you paused and chose to use your words instead of hitting or grabbing. I'm proud of you for showing that self-control in a challenging situation."* (End with a hug.)

Catching kids being good reinforces good behavior and increases the likelihood that it will be repeated. Trying to catch our kids being good also creates a mind-set that primes us to expect the positive (see #68).

TRY THIS: Be alert every day for opportunities to acknowledge (and therefore reinforce) your children's good behavior. Praise them: (1) specifically, (2) immediately, (3) sincerely, and also (4) nonverbally (e.g., with hugs and positive touch).

25

Great parents
discipline lovingly

DISCIPLINING WITH LOVE is a parenting principle that encompasses many different practices from this book. Disciplining with love means that:

- The goal is to teach (#28), not to punish or shame. When you discipline your child, keep the focus on his problematic behavior and aim for your words to reflect that you are disapproving of your child's behavior, not your child himself (see also #9 and #10). Avoid threats, emotional withdrawal, or anger.[7]
- Parents strive to remain matter-of-fact and calm (see #54) when disciplining kids.
- Discipline is done in private (#26).
- If consequences are given, they are not harsh or punitive (#51).
- Parents pay attention to their nonverbal communication, especially body language and physical interaction (#30 and #31). For example, if you are trying to take your child back to her bed in the

middle of the night and she is resisting, avoid squeezing her arm hard as an expression of your frustration (see also #38).

- Parents maintain an emotional connection with children throughout (see #39). Discipline never includes withdrawal of love or emotional manipulation.

TRY THIS: Instead of saying to your child, "What's wrong with you?" after he's done something wrong (or anything else that puts the focus on the child instead of his behavior), try this instead: *"I don't like that behavior"* or *"*[Name the behavior] *is not okay."* A full discussion of the behavior will also include empathy (#6), the rationale for why the behavior is not okay (#46), suggestions for acceptable alternative behaviors (#21 and #22), and, in some cases, fair warning of consequences (see #47).

This phrasing may sound strange at first but it makes the point clearly that you see your child as separate from his behavior (#9).

26

Great parents
discipline in private

IMAGINE YOUR CHILD has just done something stunningly unacceptable, like hitting another child. You hustle over to address the situation and start disciplining her. Hold on.

A swift response is good, since children learn best when feedback is immediate, but if the ensuing lecture to your child about her behavior is public, or it feels public to her because she thinks it may be seen or overheard, your child may miss most of what you're saying (and thus the lesson you are trying to teach her).

For many children, especially older children who care deeply about their peer groups and social image, the experience of being disciplined in public may feel embarrassing or shaming. These strong feelings can override their ability to pay attention to what you are trying to teach them.

Since the goal of discipline is learning to do better next time (#28), and learning happens best when kids are focused, discipline is best done in private.

TRY THIS: The next time you have to discipline your child, do your best to ensure that your conversation cannot be seen or overheard. Depending on where you are, you might need to walk out to the car, go outside, or go inside. Your efforts to find a private space to talk will give your child the best chance of learning from the experience.

27

Great parents

avoid disciplining when tired or hungry

"WHEN *WHO* IS tired or hungry?" you may be wondering. Either of you. If you are tired or hungry, you are more likely to lose your patience and react, instead of responding skillfully to the situation (see #11).

Similarly, when kids are tired or hungry, they won't be focused on what you are trying to teach them. Since the goal of discipline is learning (#28), be sure your kids are in a physical and mental state (e.g., well fed and rested) that will enable them to learn from mistakes and make better choices next time.

If ignoring the situation is not possible (e.g., a known rule has been broken intentionally), then use a technique I call a "placeholder" (#66) to note the issue, then address the problematic behavior after kids are fed and rested, and *everyone* is calmer.

TRY THIS: *"I noticed that you* [give a summary of the rule violation]. *We're both tired and hungry right now, so let's take care of that first and we'll discuss what happened after a snack/nap."*

28

Great parents

see the goal of discipline as learning,

not punishment

DISCIPLINE IS ULTIMATELY about learning. The English word "discipline" is derived from the Latin *disciplina*, meaning instruction or knowledge. The English word "disciple" ("a follower or student of a teacher") is derived from this same Latin root.

Since the goal of discipline is learning, discipline is not the same as punishment, which means "the infliction or imposition of a penalty as retribution for an offense." There is a huge difference between discipline and punishment.

We may not intend to punish our kids, but we must pay close attention to our own state of mind and motivation to be careful that we are acting in accordance with our intention to teach rather than punish.

If, for example, we are feeling angry or stressed when we discipline our kids, it's much more likely that we will be punitive; for example, by giving them a consequence that is disproportionate to the offense or by being physically aggressive with them (e.g., squeezing their arm a little too hard when we usher them to their room), even if we don't actually cross the line into hitting or spanking.

When we are aggressive with our kids, or give consequences that are too severe, that focuses kids' attention on our inappropriate behavior or the unfairness of our response, distracting them from the real lesson we are trying to teach them.

In contrast, when we make learning the goal of discipline, this intention can change both our approach and our mind-set. With this goal in mind, we are more likely to give fair and reasonable consequences (#51), discipline lovingly (#34), start with empathy (#6), and focus on behavior (#9).

Seeing learning as the goal of discipline also makes it more likely that our relationship with our kids will continue to thrive even when we have to enforce consequences.

TRY THIS: Set yourself the intention of using discipline as a way to facilitate your child's learning; for example, learning about boundaries, limits, respect for others, fairness, and so on.

Pay careful attention to your emotional state (see #15, 16, and 17) and resist disciplining when you are angry or stressed (see #54). In those cases, use a placeholder (#66) and return to the issue when everyone is calm.

In order to avoid giving disproportionate consequences off the cuff when you are agitated, decide in advance on a handful of consequences that are appropriate for your child in different situations. Use the guidelines for devising consequences in #51.

29

Great parents
understand that children's brains are different

Two COMMON FRUSTRATIONS of parents, especially parents of young children, is how *loooong* everything takes, and how much repetition and reminding seems to be required.

Before becoming a parent, getting out the door in the morning used to be a breeze and now it seems to take at least twice as long. Ask your toddler to put on her shoes and ten minutes later you may find her playing intently with her blocks instead, the shoes having been long forgotten. Ask your first-grader to hang up his coat when he comes home from school and you may find the coat on the floor most afternoons. Having kids is a time-intensive and repetitive project.

True, and for good reason: Children's brains are different from adult brains. In contrast to adults, who are generally able to undertake a task and stay focused, children get distracted (as we adults often perceive it). This "distractibility" causes much frustration for parents: Parents often feel they are always reminding their children to stay focused and are constantly repeating themselves.

When you notice your kids getting "distracted," remember this: Children's brains are wired for discovery and learning. Their prefrontal cortex (the seat of executive functioning, including the ability to plan and focus) is not yet fully developed. This characteristic enables them to have an exploratory and flexible brain that researchers believe is crucial to our evolution as a species. As psychologist Alison Gopnick puts it, babies and children are like the research and development department of our species. Without children and their unique brains, the cumulative learning of our species would be severely curtailed.[8]

At the same time, individual learning relies heavily on repetition. We try something, get feedback from others and/or our environment about what works and what doesn't, and try again. And again. And again. To learn, children need lots of opportunities to try, try, and try again (see #72 and #73).

Children also have less ability than adults to pay attention to their surroundings when they are focused elsewhere, an ability often referred to as peripheral awareness and commonly known as "hearing but not listening."[9] This is the phenomenon parents experience when they ask a question of their child—who may be standing right next to them—but get no response.

Parents may think they are being ignored (and therefore feel angry or frustrated) in this scenario, but in fact their child is likely experiencing "inattentional blindness"—a lack of awareness of what is happening outside of his immediate focus of attention.

So give kids the benefit of the doubt (#36) when they are distracted or seem to be ignoring you, and try the following tips.

TRY THIS: Change your perspective to see your children's "distractibility" as a critical part of their growth and development. Remind yourself that, for young children in particular, they really can't help themselves: Their brains are not yet fully wired for focused and efficient attention.

To paraphrase another useful analogy from Gopnick: Adult brains are like a flashlight, able to focus intently on a chosen area while ignoring diversions; but children's brains are like a lantern, illuminating everything as worthy of interest and attention.

When we see our children's distractibility less as an affront or inconvenience and more as a manifestation of their wonderful ability to discover and learn, that shift in our perspective can give us the extra patience we need to remind them one more time.

Similarly, when we feel ignored by our children because we just asked them to do something and they're still sitting on the floor playing (or whatever the case may be), don't assume they registered what you said, even if they are just inches away.

Instead, to ensure they are both hearing and listening:

1. Walk over to them.
2. Make gentle physical contact (e.g., a hand on their arm).
3. Get eye contact before you speak to them. For young kids, it's also helpful to crouch down at their eye level. (For better or worse, this rules out shouting up or down the stairs as an effective communication strategy.)

If that doesn't work, consider the idea that your kids might be doing an "experiment" to see what happens when they ignore you (see #34).

30

Great parents

notice what they say and how they say it

COMMUNICATION IS BOTH verbal and nonverbal. Verbal communication is the words we use, while nonverbal communication is essentially everything else: our gestures, posture, tone of voice, eye contact, facial expression, and so on.

Words are powerful (see #10), but research convincingly shows that nonverbal aspects of communication account for much of what listeners understand. Moreover, our nonverbal cues can override and even change the meaning of our words.

In short, we need to pay attention both to *what* we say and *how* we say it.

We have all experienced the power of nonverbal communication. Words that sound like praise but are delivered with sarcasm become criticism; words that sound like love but are delivered with disinterested body language suggest ambivalence instead.

Paying attention to what we say and how we say it means noticing the message we are sending not only with our words but also with our voice and body (see also #17). When the two don't match, I call this "message incongruity."

Incongruity means that things are inconsistent or out of harmony. So if our child asks if we liked his piano recital and we respond, "Yes, honey, I enjoyed it very much," but our voice doesn't match our message (e.g., our voice lacks enthusiasm) that nonverbal cue can change the meaning of our message in a way we may not intend.

Similarly, if our child asks if everything is okay and we respond, "Sure, everything's fine, honey," in a voice that is curt or aggressive or choked with tears, then the words we are using are at odds with our nonverbal communication. Over time, this incongruity can teach kids to mistrust their perceptions or even us ("I feel like something is wrong, but Mom keeps saying everything is fine"). (See also #16.)

Incongruity is not necessarily a bad thing; for example, humor is often based on playing with differences between our words and our tone of voice. The point here is just to notice both what you say *and* how you say it, and check that they are communicating what you are intending.

TRY THIS: Pay close attention to both what you say and how you say it. Ask trusted friends or family for feedback. Is what you say matched by how you say it? Do your body language and tone of voice fit your intended message?

31

Great parents

see that actions speak louder than words

MANY PARENTS, INCLUDING me, wish they could sometimes just say to their kids, "Do as I say, not as I do."
However, the behavior that we model for our kids has a
significant impact on what they learn.

Years ago, I had a patient who, in the course of our
work together, mentioned as an aside her concern about
her son's dramatic response when his team lost a soccer
game. "Whenever his team loses, he gets really upset.
Honestly, he acts like a sore loser. His dad and I have
always said that winning is not the important thing. We
are never upset when his team loses, so I just can't understand why he acts like this."

As we explored her family's attitude toward sports
and winning, she mentioned that her husband often
watches sports, and that he is a big Yankees fan. When
I asked her how her husband responded when the Yankees lost, she replied, "When the Yankees lose a game,
my husband goes bananas. He even yells at the TV
sometimes. Oh . . ."

Even though she and her husband really meant it

when they told their son that winning wasn't important, her husband's behavior when his favorite team lost told a different story. When our behavior is contrary to our words, kids get a mixed message.

Another example of this ambiguous communication is when parents tell kids that grades are not the most important thing, yet when their kids come home from school, the parents' first question might be "How did the test go?" or "Did you turn in your homework?"

Similarly, when we tell our kids that it's not okay to yell, but we later yell at them—or we continue the conversation when our kids are yelling at us (see #23 and #71)—then our behavior is contradictory to our words, so kids get a mixed message. This is also the case if we spank our kids, but tell them at other times that it's not okay to hit (their sister or brother, their friend, etc.).

Since kids learn from what they see and experience, we must be careful about the message that our behavior sends (see also #30).

TRY THIS: Make a list of the five to ten most important values you want to teach your children—for example, caring, compassion, integrity, honesty, and responsibility. For each of those values, consider both what you say to your kids and, most importantly, how you model those values in your own life.

Now the harder part: Observe your own behavior for incongruities with what you say. For example:

- Do you tell your child that winning isn't important, but yell at the TV when your favorite team misses a shot?
- Do you tell your child that sharing is fun, but walk by homeless people sitting on the sidewalk?
- Do you emphasize to your child the importance of reading, but watch TV or videos for most of the evening after work?

If you notice a behavior in your child that you find problematic, observe your own behavior closely for possible connections. (See also #3.)

32

Great parents

practice emotion coaching

MANY PARENTS EXPECT to coach their children in sports and help with schoolwork, but if you really want to have a big impact on your child's well-being and future success, help her develop her emotional intelligence through emotion coaching.

Emotional intelligence is a set of skills that enable individuals to recognize and understand their feelings and to effectively express and manage them. Together with self-awareness (#18), emotional intelligence is a cornerstone of the critical ability to respond instead of react (#11).

Kids who have learned how to recognize and manage their feelings have higher stress tolerance, better social skills, fewer behavior problems, less anxiety and depression, and a host of other advantages.[10]

Emotion coaching may be the most important activity you can do with your child.[11] Here's how:

1. Identify. Kids must know what they're feeling before they can strategize about what to do about it.

Parents can help kids identify and name their feelings by practicing empathy (#6) and perspective taking (#8), and by going beyond basic feeling words such as "mad" and "sad" to use nuanced words that communicate the broad variety of emotional experiences, such as "disappointed," "frustrated," "embarrassed," "joyful," "pensive," and so on. As emotional vocabulary increases, so does the capacity for emotional intelligence.

2. Validate. Show your kids that you understand why they might be feeling the way they are. Again, this requires empathy and perspective taking. That said, validating a feeling does not mean that you approve of the behavior that may have accompanied that feeling. You can sympathize with your child's anger (feeling) that someone snatched a toy away from him, while still disapproving of the hitting (behavior) that accompanied his feeling.

3. Coach. Discuss with your kids how they might respond differently next time to produce a more positive outcome. Advance planning and rehearsing (#73) are helpful to allow your children to practice a new response. Practicing also makes it more likely that they will use the new response in the future.

4. Manage. Techniques for managing strong feelings can be taught or reviewed in step 3 (above). Ideally, you are also modeling these emotion regulation skills in your daily life. Teach kids a variety of techniques for managing their feelings, so that instead of reacting in emotionally charged situations, kids learn how to calm themselves down so they can make thoughtful choices about how best to respond. It's hard for kids to follow through on new responses if they are in the throes of a strong feeling.

Here are a few examples of emotion regulation techniques:

- Deep breathing
- Using power poses: Power poses are body positions that can reduce stress and increase confidence, according to social psychologist Amy Cuddy. One example would be standing tall, with shoulders squared, feet apart, and hands on hips.
- Challenging negative thoughts
- Getting outside
- Talking to a trusted person
- Exercising
- Listening to music
- Visualizing positive outcomes
- Thinking about inspiring people
- Meditating or praying
- Practicing gratitude and kindness

TRY THIS: Imagine your child just did or said something that violates your rules or values. For example, your son took a ball away from another child on the playground who was refusing to share the ball with him.

Here's how emotion coaching in that scenario might sound:

1. **Identifying:** *"Honey, I heard about what happened today at school with the ball. It sounds like Henry was refusing to share the ball with you, and you got really frustrated."* (Listen.)

2. **Validating:** *"I can see why you would be really angry and frustrated since he wouldn't share, and he wasn't following the playground rules. He should have taken turns with you, and it wasn't right for him to refuse. I would have also been very frustrated in that situation."* (Listen.)

"At the same time (see #7), *even though what Henry did was not okay, it's also not okay for you to take the ball away from him, even though it should have been your turn* (focus on behavior). *If we forcefully take away something that another person has, that is disrespectful of them* (reason)."

3. **Coaching:** Wait to do this step until your child is calm and receptive. *"So, let's talk about what you could do differently in a similar situation. What ideas do you have about a better way to handle a situation that feels unfair like that?"*

4. **Managing:** Elicit your child's ideas about alternative responses, and offer your own if necessary. Then talk about the pros and cons of each. Help him pick one he thinks is best. Then rehearse it with him, and talk about emotion regulation strategies he could use to help himself stay calmer.

"Let's pretend that I'm Henry. I'm going to do what he

did, and you're going to try doing what we just talked about.
Remember to try some of the calming techniques such as deep
breathing and walking away."

Now rehearse the scene with your child one or more times, with the goal of having him practice a new way of responding to a stressful situation. This won't guarantee a different response the next time, but over time and with continued practice, your child's ability to manage his feelings and make better behavior choices will improve.

33

Great parents

promote self-control

IN THE NOW-FAMOUS "marshmallow" experiments, researchers tested preschoolers' self-control and ability to delay gratification by sitting them in a room alone with a tempting treat and measuring how long they were able to wait. Years later, those kids who resisted temptation the longest also tended to have the highest academic achievement. In fact, their ability to delay eating the marshmallow was a better predictor of their future academic success than their IQ scores.

Further research has shown that self-control also correlates highly with greater stress tolerance and concentration abilities, as well as increased empathy, better emotion regulation (see #32), and social competence.[12]

While parents who hope that their children will be high achievers often focus on tutoring, advanced classes, and more study time, the research on self-control suggests that a "backdoor" approach may be more likely to succeed and that it's also better for kids.

Instead of focusing directly on achievement per se,

we can help our children be successful by helping them practice and develop skills related to self-control.

For young kids in particular, imaginative play (see #57) is an especially critical part of practicing self-control, since during play, kids set their own rules and are motivated to respect those rules when the game is fun. As neuroscientists Sandra Aamodt and Sam Wang note in their book *Welcome to Your Child's Brain*, "To play school, you have to act like a teacher or a student, and inhibit your impulses to act like a fighter pilot or a baby. Following these rules provides children with some of their earliest experiences with controlling their behavior to achieve a desired goal."

Self-control is a skill that can be improved through practice, so be sure your child has lots of opportunities. Remember that this is not about following rules in order to please others or avoid punishment; it's about learning to control one's own impulses in order to achieve a goal. (In the marshmallow study, kids were not punished for eating the marshmallow right away, nor were they praised for waiting, but kids knew they would get a second marshmallow if they waited.)

Keep in mind that children vary in their initial ability to demonstrate self-control, so start at the level where your child is now. The goal is to help your child succeed at developing this vital skill, so focus on her progress relative to where she was before and praise her for doing better *this time*, rather than comparing her to others.

Being compared to others who are doing better, or

repeated failures because a task is too challenging, may leave kids feeling inferior and resistant to trying anymore. Instead, create a positive feedback loop based on small, incremental successes. (See also #45.)

TRY THIS: Start by ensuring that kids have ample time for self-directed play. As noted earlier, imaginative play is a crucial setting for early experiences of self-control, because the enjoyment of the game provides the motivation to try.

In addition to self-directed play, kids can also practice self-control by doing fun activities with their parents that involve some structure, such as taking turns. Aamodt and Wang suggest board games, as long as parents allow kids to monitor themselves (e.g., avoid reminding your child repeatedly that it's not her turn yet).

If kids are having a hard time controlling themselves during the game, then look for other activities that allow them to have a successful experience of self-control based on their current skill level.

As your children get older, remember that successfully practicing self-control begets greater self-control. Researchers liken developing self-control to developing a muscle—the more we do it, the better we get.[13]

Another factor that contributes to children's self-control is warm and affectionate parenting—see #19, 39, and 74 for more details and tips.

See also #11 and #13.

34

Great parents

view kids as little explorers and scientists

MUCH OF WHAT looks like "bad" behavior is really just exploration and experimentation. Kids are naturally curious and it's their job to figure out how the world works and how to get what they want or need. Like scientists, they do "experiments."[14]

In my view, these "experiments" are in two primary domains: the natural world and the social world. The natural world includes what adults generally think of as physics (the water will spill if you invert an open cup), chemistry (when you pour milk into Mom's beer it makes an interesting mixture), civil engineering (when you flush Dad's ring down the toilet it disappears and does not return), and so on.

Think of the world from your child's perspective: If you weren't yet familiar with gravity, you might also keep dropping or pouring things to see if they will go down every time. Kids really do experience the world in a different way than adults (see also #29).

The second domain—the social world—is where the action really is. Experiments in the social world focus on the important people in children's lives: parents, siblings, family members, caregivers, and teachers. Kids need to know how each of these people work and how to get what they need or want from them: love, affection, five more minutes at the playground, ice cream, screen time, privacy, and so on.

The answer to these critical questions (How do you work? What happens if I _____? How do I get _____ from you?) varies from person to person. To get the answers, kids must do "experiments" on us, experiments we often think of as "testing." When your child appears to be misbehaving, I encourage you to imagine her wearing a tiny white lab coat and taking notes about the results of her experiment (on you) in an imaginary lab notebook: *When I throw a tantrum in public, I'm more likely to get what I want than if I do the same at home. Interesting . . ."*

If what we want kids to know about us is that we mean what we say, that we can be relied on to do what we say we're going to do, that we are fair and reasonable, and so on, then we need to teach them this through our daily interactions with them.

Seeing our children's behavior through this lens—as an experiment aimed at getting useful information about how people and the world work—can also help us not to take it personally when they push our buttons or ignore us.

TRY THIS: The next time you find yourself dealing with your child's challenging behavior, change your lens to see it as an experiment intended to get useful information about how things work (in the world or in your family) and respond accordingly.

Ask yourself this crucial question: "What do I want my kids to know about me?"

Write down two or three words (e.g., "kind," "patient," "fun," "reasonable," "centered," "reliable") that you would like your children to think of when they think of you.

Now try to see yourself from your children's perspective. How might they view you? Do those qualities match the ones you would like for them to associate with you?

For each word that you choose above, write down two or three *specific* behaviors relevant to your life that would clearly demonstrate those qualities to your kids in your regular interactions with them and others. Here's an example for "reliable."

Reliable:

1. When my daughter asks me to play with her, and I tell her that I will in one minute, I will stop what I'm doing in one minute and follow through on that commitment. (See also #1.)

2. I will not tell my kids that we will go to the movies (or the park, or whatever) next weekend unless I am willing and able to make that happen.
3. When my son wants to show me the new trick he learned in skateboarding, I will not say, "Sure, after I finish this report!" without also making a note to remind myself to follow up with him later that day.

The final step is to implement those new behaviors purposefully in your daily life. Pick one specific behavior per week, and put it into practice. Add a new one each week until these behaviors become part of your regular way of interacting with your kids. (See also #20.)

35

Great parents
give previews

A PREVIEW IS sharing your knowledge and experience with your kids, without insisting that they make the same choices that you would.

Previews go hand in hand with allowing natural consequences (#50); together, they are a powerful way to minimize power struggles (#61) and give your kids autonomy (see #13 and #37).

TRY THIS: Imagine your daughter is insisting on taking her new train set to the park, an idea that you oppose because you suspect parts of it will get lost or damaged (and then she'll be upset). Rather than get into a power struggle about bringing the toy ("No, you can't bring the train set, it might get lost or damaged"), give your daughter a preview (your best guess about what's going to happen—that is, the natural consequence) and also make it clear that *she* can make the choice.*

---

* Unless there is a risk to health or safety, or if the natural consequence of her choice isn't hers to bear. For example, if the train set actually belongs to her brother, then bringing it to the park is not her choice to make.

"Sweetie, I can see that you really want to bring your train set with us to the park (empathy, #6). *I think that if you bring it to the park where there are going to be lots of other kids playing, part of the set might get lost or damaged* (preview). *I wouldn't bring a special toy to the park if it were mine, but it's up to you* (power sharing). *We're leaving in two minutes, so please decide if you want to bring it or not."*

If she decides to bring the train set to the park and, as you suspected, it gets lost or damaged (and she runs to you crying), resist the urge to say "I told you so!" or promise to buy her a new one. Instead, start with empathy (#6) and then matter-of-factly review (#54) what happened and discuss what choices your daughter could make differently next time.

"Oh, honey, your caboose got a big dent and a scratch on it. I know that's so upsetting for you! (Hug.) *That's the downside of bringing a special toy to a big park. Next time we come to the park, do you think you'll want to bring a special toy again?"*

On the next occasion that she wants to bring a toy or other item somewhere (and you think it is a bad idea), gently remind her of the train experience: *"I see you want to bring* [name item] *with you on our camping trip. That's up to you. I remember a few months ago when you brought the train set to the park and later wished you hadn't because it got damaged. There's a chance that might happen again with* [name item], *but it's yours so you can decide."*

36

Great parents

give kids the benefit of the doubt

WHEN THEIR KIDS don't follow the rules or otherwise disappoint them with a given behavior, great parents strive to convey, both in what they say and how they say it, that they view their kids as works in progress who have the intention to do better.[15]

Kids whose parents frequently criticize, blame, or suggest that their children are flawed ("What's wrong with you?" "You're making me crazy!" "That's ridiculous!" "You always ____," "You never ____") tend to experience greater depression and anxiety and exhibit more aggression and impaired social skills.[16] (See also #10.)

In contrast, great parents pay attention both to *what* they say (their words) and *how* they say it (their nonverbal communication; see also #30 and #31). They avoid sarcasm, eye rolling, yelling, and aggressive behavior. When presented with a parenting challenge (such as whining, tantrums, hitting, uncooperativeness, etc.), they focus on their child's behavior, instead of their child's sense of self.

Great parents intentionally view their children through a positive lens. This doesn't mean that they have rose-colored glasses and see their children as doing no wrong. Rather, it means that these parents view misbehavior and mistakes as an inevitable part of a long-term process of learning and improvement. They see their kids as being "under construction" and maintain optimism about their kids' ability to do better with practice and support.

TRY THIS: The next time you are confronted with some childhood misdeed (e.g., your daughter has been caught cheating), remember to preface your conversation with her by reminding yourself that she is a work in progress with the intent to do better.

Many of the practices in this book can help you do this, such as these:

- Separate her behavior (cheating) from her sense of self (#9).
- Empathize with her goals (her desire to do well on the test) while discussing why her method (cheating) is problematic (#21).
- Discuss alternative methods (#22).
- Give appropriate consequences (#51).
- Stay matter-of-fact (#54).
- Maintain a strong emotional connection (#39).
- Teach emotion regulation skills (#32).

37

Great parents

share their power

HAVE YOU EVER had an insufferable boss: one who told you what to do, how to do it, and when to do it? Not only that, but this person also controlled your paycheck, and you didn't have any other options?

If you have, then you know something about what it's like to be a child with a parent who allows little or no autonomy. Controlling parents give kids little independence to make their own choices, often with the well-intentioned goal of protecting their kids from mistakes or discomfort. But this approach has hidden perils of its own (see #13, on over-functioning).

In many families, parents control all the resources (though less so as kids get older). Therefore, the primary source of power that kids have is their emotional bond with parents: the fact that their parents love them and want to be loved in return.

If kids don't perceive that their family operates in a reasonable, fair, and thoughtful way, they may turn to emotional tactics to get what they want, such as "You never understand!" and "I hate you!" Or, they may pretend to comply with a controlling parent's wishes, and then covertly do it their own way.

Great parents share their power with kids in age- and development-appropriate ways, with children gaining more power and autonomy as they demonstrate ability and responsibility. Children whose parents give them more autonomy have better relationships with their parents over time and tend to view parents more positively.[17] Children given more autonomy also develop greater self-control,[18] which has a host of other benefits (see #33).

So show your kids through your interactions with them that the way to get more independence is to behave in a way that merits it.

TRY THIS: If you find yourself dictating to your children how they should do something that they are capable of deciding for themselves, back off and let them try. They will learn by trying, making mistakes, and trying again. (See also #50.)

For example, if it's raining outside and your daughter insists on wearing her sandals instead of her rain boots, consider letting her.* Rather than get into a power

---

* Unless you live in a cold climate, it's wintertime, and her choice may lead to frostbite or worse. This raises an important exception to this principle: If your child's choice may pose a risk to her or anyone else's health or safety, then it's not an option. In those cases: Start with empathy (#6), then be authoritative (see #38), give a reason (see #46), and possibly try distraction and/or humor (#69), which are most effective with younger kids. For ongoing issues (e.g., refusing the car seat), try rehearsals (#73).

struggle about the sandals (or whatever the issue is), give your daughter a matter-of-fact preview (#35)—your best guess about what's going to happen (cold and wet feet) and then make it clear that the choice is up to her. This is a magical combination.

Here's how that might sound in practice: *"Sweetie, I can see that you really want to wear your sandals today even though it's raining outside* (empathy). *I think if you do that, your feet will get cold and wet so I don't recommend it* (preview), *but it's up to you* (power sharing). *Please decide and let's be ready to go in five minutes."*

If your daughter doesn't like the experience of cold and wet feet, she is unlikely to make the same choice again. (Note that her not liking the experience of having cold and wet feet is not the same thing as you not liking it for her.)

38

Great parents
are in charge

THE IDEA OF being in charge might seem contradictory to the previous principle (#37) of sharing your power with kids. However, being in charge—what I'll call an authoritative style—means being comfortable with your power as a parent so that you can both use and share that power.

In contrast to an authoritarian style ("My way or the highway" or "Because I said so") or a permissive style ("Whatever you want" or "Never mind, if you just don't want to"), an authoritative style[19] strikes the right balance between being responsive to children's needs while also setting firm, fair limits.

Being authoritative means giving children developmentally appropriate autonomy to make choices and mistakes. Being authoritative means you are warm but not indulgent, firm but not forceful.

In this style of parenting, discipline is done with the goal of teaching, not punishment (#28), and is focused specifically on the child's behavior rather than the qualities of the child (#9).

Here are some examples of *not* being authoritative:

- Trying to avoid making your child angry or upset by not enforcing a rule he knows but doesn't like
- Joining your teenager and her friends in social activities as one of the gang
- Using physical force or aggressiveness to get your kids to do what you ask
- Giving a toddler on the verge of a tantrum what he wants in order to keep the peace

In contrast, authoritative parents strive to be matter-of-fact, firm, reasonable, fair, consistent, predictable, affectionate, and empathic. Many parenting practices that support an authoritative style are summarized in this book.

Importantly, authoritative parents avoid using shame ("What's wrong with you?"), blame ("You're making me crazy!"), or fear ("You'd better ____ or else!") to establish and enforce rules (see #10). Instead, they are matter-of-fact (#54) and rely on reasons (#46), consistency (#53), empathy (#6), and fair warning (#47). They also focus on the relationship (#74) and maintain a warm and affectionate attitude (#39).

TRY THIS: Being authoritative is a general parenting style, composed of many interrelated parenting behaviors. Review the practices listed above to see examples of what to say and do to create a more authoritative style.

39

Great parents

maintain a warm and affectionate attitude

BEING WARM AND affectionate with your child is easy when family life is humming along harmoniously, but it can be much more difficult when kids are pushing limits or behaving badly. However, if we withdraw emotionally from kids as a way of expressing our anger or frustration, then we are using love as a method of coercion and punishment: *I love you only if you act the way I want.* This is conditional love.

Instead, the message we want to send to our kids is this: *I love you all the time, even when I don't like your behavior.* It's important to keep our emotional connection with kids strong even—and especially—when we set limits, enforce boundaries, and give consequences.

Trust, respect, and a strong emotional connection are the foundations of a good relationship, and a good relationship is the foundation of a happy and harmonious family life (see #74). Moreover, research suggests that parental warmth can help protect kids from long-term effects of childhood stress.[20]

Note that being warm and affectionate is not the same thing as being permissive or indulgent. Being warm and affectionate does not mean that we give in to our children's unreasonable demands or allow them to behave inappropriately.

Instead, the goal is to maintain a warm and affectionate attitude while also enforcing firm and reasonable rules and expectations for behavior.

Most of the practices in this book are intended to help you navigate this balance. For example: practicing empathy (#6) and positive touch (#19), striving to be matter-of-fact (#54), accepting kids as they are (#9), separating your children from their behavior (#11), disciplining with love (#25), being in charge (#38), and catching kids being good (#24).

TRY THIS: Remind yourself that who your child is as a person is not the same as his behavior. Focus your love and affection on your child's personhood, while matter-of-factly dealing with his problematic behavior. Remember that discipline can be done in a loving way.

Imagine you have just disciplined your child and he has angrily retreated to his room, maybe even slamming the door to signal his extreme frustration. Bedtime is coming up, and it's your habit to tuck him in and give him a goodnight kiss. Should you skip that tonight, since he's so upset with you (and you with him)? No, for the reasons given above.

Instead, stick to your usual routine and make an effort to maintain the emotional connection. What if, when you enter the room, he tells you to go away or resists your attempts to give him a goodnight kiss? Don't force the issue but do calmly make it clear that you would still like to tuck him in. Demonstrate through what you say and do that you see the event that gave rise to the discipline as a temporary blip in the context of a long and loving relationship.

"Honey, I know you are very angry right now and it seems like you don't want me to give you a goodnight kiss. Are you sure? OK, then, I love you and I'll see you in the morning."

Great parents
treat their kids with respect, consideration, and kindness

MOST PARENTS EXPECT their kids to say "please" and "thank you" and use other conversational niceties when speaking to them or other adults.

However, many of these same parents do not regularly say "please" and "thank you" when speaking to their children, often because they forget, and in some cases because they view it as a prerogative of parental authority to simply give orders (but see #37).

If we want our children to learn nice manners, and behave well in stressful situations, then we need to model it for them, not only in our interactions with others but also in our daily interactions with them. Similarly, if we frequently yell at our children, we are implicitly teaching them that yelling is an acceptable way to communicate.

This principle goes hand in hand with the one following (#41).

TRY THIS: Pay attention to the ways in which you speak to and behave with your children. Observe what kind of behavior you are modeling for them. If you don't already do so, make an effort to say "please" and "thank you" regularly when you speak to them or ask them to do something for you.

Another way to identify areas in which you can teach by example is to turn the tables. If your child adopted your behaviors, would you be pleased? (See also #3.)

Great parents

expect their kids to treat them with respect, consideration, and kindness

ALTHOUGH ALMOST EVERY parent would agree that their kids should treat them with respect, consideration, and kindness, and are also vigilant about how their kids treat others, it's surprising how many parents unintentionally allow their children to treat *them* poorly.

You can observe examples of this on a daily basis: kids who interrupt their parents; kids who speak disrespectfully to their parents; kids who yell at, hit, or push their parents or pull their hair.

While parents rarely allow their kids to behave this way with others, parents unintentionally allow their kids to treat them poorly for a number of reasons:

- Parents are not paying attention to the situation and don't notice the behavior.
- Parents are used to the behavior.
- Parents don't know how to change the behavior.
- The behavior fits parents' expectation of how kids behave.

- Parents see tolerating such behavior as an expression of how much they love their kids.

Whatever the reason, allowing your kids to treat you poorly is not only establishing a dysfunctional pattern of behavior (see #20), it also makes it more likely that your kids will treat others that way, too.

As an example, imagine a loving mom who is considerate of her son but notices that other children complain about how he treats them. She knows that she is treating her son with respect and kindness (see #40), but doesn't notice that she unintentionally allows her son to interrupt her frequently and yell at her or push her when he is angry.

TRY THIS: Pay attention to how your child interacts with *you*. If you notice any behavior with you that you would not want to see duplicated with others, stop the action (#71) and matter-of-factly (#54) point out the behavior. Describe why it's problematic, and ask for a replay (#72). Do not gratify the behavior (#23). Stage a rehearsal (#73). Give the rule and your rationale (#46) and fair warning (#47) if necessary.

42

Great parents

rarely say "Good job!"
or "You are so smart!"

It makes intuitive sense that praising our children for being wonderful, special, and talented would help them to be confident and have healthy self-esteem, but in fact, many studies convincingly show that nonspecific, ability-focused, and excessive praise can actually have the opposite effect, influencing children to develop what pioneering psychologist Carol Dweck calls a "fixed" mind-set.

As Dweck explains: "In a fixed mind-set students believe their basic abilities, their intelligence, their talents, are just fixed traits. They have a certain amount and that's that, and then their goal becomes to look smart all the time and never look dumb."[21] Children who have a fixed mind-set often become reluctant to take risks or try new activities, for fear of "looking dumb" or losing their status as special and talented.

However, Dweck's research identifies a different mind-set that can be cultivated by teaching kids that intelligence and ability are flexible qualities that can be developed through hard work and perseverance.

She calls this a "growth" mind-set: "In a growth

mind-set students understand that their talents and abilities can be developed through effort, good teaching and persistence. They don't necessarily think everyone's the same or anyone can be Einstein, but they believe everyone can get smarter if they work at it."[22] Kids who have a growth mind-set see failure as part of the process of learning (see #13), and their successes as directly tied to their effort and persistence.

One way that parents and other adults can help kids develop a growth mind-set is through praise. To promote a growth mind-set, praise should be *specific* and focused on the *effort* children put into the process, rather than on outcomes or abilities—this sort of specific and effort-focused praise facilitates development of a growth mind-set.

"Good job" is a perfect example of nonspecific praise. Although positive, "Good job" does not tell children anything specific about what they did to earn the compliment. Many parents use "Good job," and other similar phrases, indiscriminately throughout the day to remark on children's (often unremarkable) achievements.

Another kind of praise that also has unintended negative effects is outcome- or trait-based compliments, such as "You are so smart," "You are so good at _____," or any compliment that focuses attention on what the child is, instead of what they specifically did to earn the praise.

The bottom line: Use praise to communicate the idea

that success is something kids can influence through hard work and perseverance.*

TRY THIS: Pay close attention to how and when you praise your child. Avoid saying "Good job!" unless you also pair it with a specific statement of what kind of effort your child put forth to earn your praise.

Similarly, avoid praise that focuses on ability, such as, "You are so smart/talented/good at _____."

For example, rather than saying, "Good job, you got two As on your report card!" you might say instead: *"Hey, I noticed you've been working hard and staying focused in history and algebra. All those extra problem sets you've been doing have obviously been paying off. I know how frustrating it was for you at the beginning of the year, and I'm really proud of your effort and perseverance."*

And what if you know that your child didn't work very hard for those As? In that case, you might not say much at all, or you might challenge your child to improve in an area that doesn't come so easily. For exam-

---

* Although focusing on hard work is a cornerstone of Dweck's approach to developing a growth mind-set, Dweck herself notes that it is not only about effort. She points out that while effort is critical to learning, it is not equivalent to learning, which is the ultimate goal. For that, students must also seek guidance when they are no longer making progress, and also be willing to try new strategies. Think of it this way: If a student is pushing with all his might on a brick wall with the goal of getting to the other side, it would not help him achieve that goal to praise him for how hard he is pushing. Instead, he needs someone to help him consider another way (e.g., climbing over or digging under) and then he must try it.

ple: "*I see you got another A in algebra. I wonder if you need more challenges in your math class? You also went from a B− to a B+ in English. I'm really proud of the progress you've made there. I noticed you were putting a lot of extra time and effort into your book reports, and it shows. Well done!*"

43

Great parents
(mostly) avoid labels

PICTURE THIS COMMONPLACE scene: As a mom walks into a crowded room with her young son (maybe another child's birthday party), he holds tightly onto her leg, resisting his mother's attempts to get him to say hello or play with the other children. "He's just shy," she remarks to another mom who walks over to greet them.

It sounds innocuous but, repeated over time, this kind of label often starts to stick. It can lead others to describe her child as such, and also make her son see himself this way. Whether you consider shyness to be "good" or "bad" is not really the issue—the issue is that labels like this impose a characteristic on someone from the outside and imply that that characteristic is fixed. (For the record, I don't view shyness negatively.)

Even some labels that many parents would feel good about using (e.g., "She is so smart") are problematic, because they send the message to kids that that trait is an innate and fixed quality that is part of that child's identity, for better or for worse.

If the label is seen as positive, the child's perspective

may become "I am smart/creative/good at sports and I want to stay that way" (i.e., keep the label). This perspective is associated with a "fixed" mind-set in which children tend to avoid risks or the possibility of failure, which might cause them to lose their positive label.

If the label is seen as negative, the child's perspective may become "I am shy/hyper/bad at drawing and I don't want to be." In this case, the label is an implicit criticism of the child that she may come to associate with who she is, rather than see the behavior described by the label as changeable and subject to her personal control.

That said, when it comes to promoting moral and pro-social behavior (such as helping, caring, and sharing), then certain labels may be useful. For example, research has found that children who are asked to "be a helper" (instead of just being asked to help) are significantly more likely to pitch in on a shared task, like cleaning up toys.

In reality, most common labels like "shy" or "smart" are not static and stable qualities, but are behaviors that are context-dependent and changeable. In the case of smartness, we know that kids can show smartness in one area but not another, and that smartness can also be increased through effort and persistence (see #42). In the case of shyness, children can exhibit shyness in one setting but not another, and research also shows that about half of children who exhibit shyness at an early age do not still act shy by age ten.[23]

TRY THIS: Pay attention to how you describe your children to others and to your children themselves. Try changing your language to convey the message that their behavior is not their identity.

For example, instead of saying "He's just shy," you might say: "He's feeling shy right now." In the second phrase, shyness is not a label, but instead describes your child's behavior or feelings at that moment in time.

This small change in language implies that shyness is not a "forever" quality and gives kids more freedom to behave differently at other times and in other situations.

However, if you are trying to encourage helping, caring, or sharing behavior, then consider using words that describe a positive character, as opposed to just behavior. For example: *"Please be a helper"* or *"You are a caring/ helpful/generous person."*

44

Great parents
play it straight

IN OUR PARENTING life, we are often presented with a dilemma: Do I answer my children honestly when they ask me a question, or do I fudge for the sake of their confidence, enjoyment, peace of mind, or some other value?

Children ask a lot of questions (see #34) and parents can feel put on the spot: "Am I a good dancer/artist/baseball player?" "Are you getting a divorce/having another baby/losing your job?" "Do you believe in God/think I look good in this dress/think I'm smart?"

How to respond? Consider playing it straight, with allowances for your child's developmental stage and your personal values. Kids don't need to know all the nitty-gritty details, but based on their age and maturity, you can decide on the right level of candor.

Playing it straight is also part of teaching kids that they can trust us to be honest, and it also encourages them to seek our opinion since they expect we will respond as truthfully as we can.

Most parents are inevitably biased toward their children—and this is generally a good thing—but children whose parents are overly praising ("You are the best artist I've ever seen!") or evasive ("Don't worry about my job, honey; I've got it under control") may eventually discount or mistrust their parents' words and opinions. Kids who are overly praised, for example, may come to the conclusion that you have low expectations of them (see #42). Excessive praise may also give kids an inflated view of their skills, which can cause distress when they later make real-world comparisons.

TRY THIS: Your eight-year-old son asks: "Do you think I'm a good soccer player?" This is a golden opportunity to answer truthfully and also to emphasize the importance of effort and practice.

Instead of just saying, "Yes, you're awesome!" you might say something like this: "Given the amount of time you spend practicing and how much effort you put into developing your soccer skills, you are making good progress. Your dribbling skills have really come a long way since you started."

Here's a different example: "Are you getting divorced?" asks your five-year-old daughter. Instead of being evasive, answer as truthfully as possible, while omitting unnecessary details, depending on your child's age and level of maturity.

You might first respond with "Why do you ask?" This question is a good way to understand your child's motivation behind the question: Is she worried about where she will live or which school she will attend? Is she looking for an explanation for the increase in arguments around the house? Or something else?

Once you know why your child is asking, you can address your response to her specific concerns. For example: "Mom and I have been talking about that possibility but we haven't decided yet. When we do decide, we will let you know right away. Even if we do decide to separate, you would still stay in your current school."

45

Great parents
use scaffolding

THE CONCEPT OF scaffolding can help parents decide how to support kids when they ask for help or need it. Since parents must be cautious to avoid over-functioning for kids (#13), scaffolding is an approach that allows parents to offer assistance without taking over.[24]

Wikipedia defines scaffolding as a "temporary structure used to support a work crew and materials to aid in the construction, maintenance and repair of buildings." The key words in this definition are "temporary," "support," and "aid." The scaffolding is not the building itself. It is there temporarily to support the workers who are doing the actual work of building.

Similarly, parents can provide support and assistance in many different areas of their children's lives (scaffolding), while avoiding doing the work itself (building).

For example, if your child is struggling with his math homework ("Mom, what's nine divided by four as a fraction?"), it can be tempting to jump in and give him the answer ("Two and one-fourth"). But giving him the answer will not help your child in the long term (see #4).

Conversely, it's probably not helpful to respond with, "Keep working; you'll figure it out."

The middle ground would be to use a scaffolding approach. In this approach, you would offer assistance while still letting your child do the substantive work: "Okay, so what's the closest number to nine that you can easily divide by four?" And again, if necessary, you would further break the problem down: "And what's the difference between that number and nine?"

With scaffolding, less is more. Provide as much support as your child needs in order to be successful and move on to the next incremental skill level.* The idea is to focus on one small step at a time.

If you don't notice small positive steps that you can praise, read about rehearsals (#73) for more details on how to create those opportunities.

TRY THIS: The goal of scaffolding is to help your children practice and develop their skills in various areas of life, from schoolwork and chores to time management and organization.

The next time your child asks for or needs help to accomplish something that requires skill, step back and

---

* But in situations where your children just need a helping hand (e.g., they spilled a gallon of milk on the floor) you can just jump in and be helpful instead of wondering how your assistance will affect their ability to build their skills. In this case, your behavior is modeling the importance of being helpful and supportive.

ask yourself how the task or project might be broken down into smaller steps, and which steps your child is capable of doing independently, or with your support.

For example, if you want your elementary-school-aged daughter to get herself ready for school, instead of just reminding her of what to do every morning, or presenting her with a checklist, you might ask her to imagine a typical morning. Ask her to narrate all the things she usually does before leaving for school. As she is talking, you can write, or better yet, ask her to write down those items (get dressed, eat breakfast, brush teeth, etc.). Or ask her to draw pictures of each task, if she is not yet reading and writing.

Prompt her as needed if she overlooks any important items: *"And are there any things you need to bring with you to school? Yes? Okay, what are some examples? Yes, right, returning your school library books every Friday. Let's write that down, too."*

The goal is to walk her through the process of organizing her morning and creating her own reminders. In so doing, she will begin to learn how to get organized, and she is also more likely to follow reminders that she herself created.

46

Great parents

give a reason

In our busy lives as parents, we may not even notice ourselves barking out dos and don'ts to our kids: "Get your shoes on now," "Turn off the computer," "Stop that," and so on. Then we may get frustrated when our kids seem to ignore us or resist doing what we've asked.

Here again, we have the beginnings of a power struggle (see #61). But we may be able to sidestep it if we help our kids understand *why* we are asking—that is, if we give them a reason to go with our request.

Note: "Because I said so" or "Because I'm your father/mother" is not a reason (and often leads to power struggles or secrecy).

For younger kids in particular, many of our rules and requests can seem arbitrary—for example, "Don't pour your milk on the table" or "Don't sit on the dog." Pouring milk and watching it spread into a small puddle on the table is fun (especially if you don't have to clean it up) and sitting on the dog can be an adventure (if you don't realize that it might hurt the dog or provoke him to bite).

Talking about the reason behind a rule or request

will help kids learn to consider the effects of their behavior and choices. Adapt your reason to fit your child's developmental stage, so that a two-year-old gets a more simplified explanation than a twelve-year-old.

An important benefit of giving a reason to go with our rule or request is that it forces us to consider our own rationale for it. In some cases, we may be insisting on things being a certain way without having really considered why it must be so. Do our kids really have to brush their hair every day or wear matching shoes? That's up to you, but remember that if you set a rule you need to enforce it consistently (#53). How do you want to spend your time?

Considering the rationales for our rules can help us to decide which rules are most important and pare them down to just the essentials. Reducing the number of household rules to only those that really matter has a host of benefits: it gives our kids more autonomy (#37), reduces power struggles, and gives us less to enforce.

Note that the best reasons generally invoke health or safety, the needs and feelings of others (e.g., the dog being sat upon or the adult who has to wipe up the table), and/or the longer-term impact of an action.

This technique does not guarantee immediate compliance with your rules and requests (see #29 and #34), but it will show your kids that you aim to be reasonable and, more importantly, it models the importance of using good reasons to motivate behavior.*

---

* But note that reasoning isn't always the best strategy (see #49).

———

TRY THIS: Whenever you state a rule or make a request, include a brief reason that fits your child's developmental stage. I call this technique "R/R" (Request/Reason).

Instead of saying "Please go get your shoes on now," you would say: *"Please go get your shoes on now* (request). *We have to leave in two minutes or we'll be late to pick up your friends for soccer practice* (reason)."

Great parents
give fair warning

GIVING FAIR WARNING is a cornerstone of the approach to loving discipline that I teach in my workshops. Because we want our children to learn that behavior is a choice, we need to tell them *in advance* the consequences for breaking a rule or ignoring a request.

This principle goes hand in hand with the one preceding (#46). Once kids know the rules and the reason for the rules, they also need to know what will happen if they choose to break the rules (or ignore your request). This is the principle of "fair warning," which applies when parents must create and give consequences (instead of relying on natural consequences, which are generally preferable—see #50).

Fair warning is a key part of an effective discipline strategy because if children know *in advance* what the consequences are for breaking a rule, then they are making a *choice* about their behavior: whether they are going to follow the rule, or break the rule and accept the consequences. There are no surprises. Fair warning also emphasizes the related principle that behavior is a choice (see #11).

One important implication of the principle of fair warning is this: If children are not aware of the rule (however obvious it may seem to you), then there should be no consequence.

For example, if little Billy decides that drawing on your new couch with a crayon would be interesting, remember that he is primarily out to explore and engage with his environment (see #34). Pause and take a deep breath if you feel angry (see #15 and #16) and then matter-of-factly (see #54) respond with the rule, the reason, and the consequence for next time. An example of this is given in the "Try This" section.

One question that often comes up is how fair warning is different from a threat. There are three crucial differences: (1) the nature of the consequences, (2) how those consequences are communicated and enforced, and (3) consistency. In short, the consequence should fit the crime, so to speak (i.e., do not give your child a severe consequence just because you are in a bad mood), and consequences should be enforced matter-of-factly and consistently. See #51 and #53 for more information.

Another common question about giving fair warning is how often you need to repeat it. The answer depends on the age and developmental stage of your child. Younger children will need more repeated reminders (see #29). If you're not sure, give your children the benefit of the doubt (see #36) and remind them again.

That said, if you have clearly communicated and discussed your rules and values, and your eight-year-old surreptitiously uses your credit card online to buy a pair of shoes he wants, then there is no need for further reminders before giving a reasonable consequence, even if he's never done exactly that before. (But do be sure to have another discussion with your child about why his behavior was unacceptable.)

Bottom line: Don't discipline children unless they *knowingly* break a rule or *intentionally* ignore a reasonable request.

TRY THIS: *"Honey, I know it seems fun to draw on the couch* (empathy), *and when you do that it's hard to remove and can damage the couch* (reason). *If you draw on the couch, then I will take the crayons away until I can be sure you know where it's okay to draw"* (or: *"until I can sit with you while you are drawing"). If you're not sure what's OK to draw on, just ask."*

Then supervise Billy closely when he is using his crayons and be ready to redirect him matter-of-factly when he heads for something you don't want subjected to his artistic efforts.

If you do take the crayons away, keep it brief (a few minutes) and then offer your child a replay (see #72). If he keeps heading toward the couch with the crayons after several replays, put the crayons away for the rest of the day and try again tomorrow with supervision, offering lots of specific praise (#42) when he does keep the crayons off the furniture (e.g. *"Billy, I love to see you using your crayons on the paper and cardboard, and really appreciate you keeping them off the furniture. Thanks, sweetie!"*).

48

Great parents

are transparent about their decision-making process

FOR MANY KIDS, parents' decisions can seem like they come out of a proverbial black box: "Yes, you can go to the party" or "No, you can't buy that toy." Decisions are handed down without giving kids an understanding of how they were made. When this happens routinely, kids may start to perceive parents as unfair and unreasonable, and parents also miss the opportunity to show kids what happens "under the hood": how to gather reasons, weigh options and priorities, come to a decision, and take action.

Part of being transparent about how you make a decision is giving a reason (#46) and another part is narrating your internal process. So if you tell your twelve-year-old that she can't go to the sleepover, give her the reason and also explain how that reason fits into your final decision: *"I know you really want to go to Annie's sleepover and it's upsetting to think you might miss it* (empathy, #6). *At the same time, you've been up late every night this week and I don't want you to have another really late night* (reason/process). *If you want to go to more sleepovers, please help me make sure you are getting at least nine hours of sleep every night* (give alternative, #22)."

Another benefit of being transparent about your decisions is that it paves the way for you to change your mind. This book emphasizes the importance of doing what you say (#1) and following through consistently (#53). But what if, for example, you tell your daughter that she can't go to the sleepover and then you change your mind?

You might have a good reason for changing your mind, but if you don't tell her about it explicitly, it may appear that you changed your mind in response to, for example, your daughter's outburst when she found out she couldn't go ("You don't get it! You are the worst mom ever!"). If so, that would increase the likelihood of your daughter using that tactic again to get her desired outcome (see #21 and #23).

Instead, you might say: *"Honey, I know you are very disappointed that you can't go to the sleepover* (empathy). *If you'd like to talk about my concerns about your sleep, I am willing to reconsider* (replay, #72)."

From the ensuing conversation, one compromise might be for you to allow her to go and see her friends for part of the evening, while planning to pick her up so she can go to bed on time at home. Or you might propose an early-start sleepover at your house instead, so that you can better monitor bedtimes.

The exact resolution is less important than the process, with the goal of your daughter seeing that the decision is grounded in thoughtful reasoning (even if she doesn't agree with it).

TRY THIS: When you are making a decision that has an outcome important to your child, make an effort to explain why and how you came to your decision. If you decide to change your mind, explain that process, too.

49

Great parents

know that reasoning has its limits

As IMPORTANT AS it is to use reasoning as the underpinning for our rules, requests, and discipline (see #46), reasoning has its limits.

If you've ever tried to reason with a child who was emotionally distraught or in the throes of a tantrum, you know what I mean: It rarely works to calm a child down by explaining to him why he shouldn't be upset or why he received the consequence that provoked the tantrum.

Trying to reason with a child (or adult) in a highly emotional state is likely to exacerbate the problem rather than alleviate it. In these situations, reasoning needs to be temporarily set aside.

When strong emotions are involved, reasoning tends to be ineffective. Emotions are always part of our thinking and decision-making processes, but when we are in a highly emotional or depleted state, they can effectively drown out our ability to think clearly and rationally, leading us to do and say things we may later regret. This is true for both adults and children.

In these emotionally charged situations, the best approach is to start from feelings, rather than reason. One of the best tools to do this is empathy (see #6).

We must pay attention to what is happening in the moment (#17), so that we can notice that the situation calls for empathy (feeling) instead of reasoning (thinking).

Note, too, that reasoning is not the most effective way to change behavior—instead try replays (#72) and rehearsals (#73).

TRY THIS: In our parenting lives, this principle means that we meet feelings with feelings. If our child is getting upset or heading toward a meltdown, we attend to her feelings instead of trying to reason her out of it. We temporarily set reasoning aside.

For example, imagine your twelve-year-old daughter is getting ready for school but she apparently can't decide what to wear. She's already changed outfits three times, and she's still not happy with her clothes. You can tell she's getting more and more upset, even though you think all her discarded outfits look nice. She complains, "This looks terrible. I don't have anything to wear. I hate my clothes."

It can be extremely tempting in this moment to explain that she has dozens of outfits, that you worked hard to have the money to pay for her clothes, that she looks nice in all of them, and so on, but any of those responses, albeit true, is likely to escalate the situation. Save them for later.

Instead, if your goal is to de-escalate the situation and get your daughter to move past the clothes issue, focus on feelings. *"It sounds like you're really not liking any of your clothes right now. Sorry, honey."* If you can think of similar situations from your own experience, you might add that, too: *"The other night when I went out to dinner with friends, I just couldn't find an outfit that I wanted to wear, and it was really frustrating."*

After that, if the moment feels right, try to change the subject and shift the attention to a neutral subject: *"So, do you want peanut butter or honey on your toast?"*

50

Great parents
harness the power of natural consequences

LET KIDS EXPERIENCE the natural consequences of their actions and choices. This is essential to learning.

Kids (and adults) learn best from experience. We can share with kids our "lessons learned," and some kids will listen and take these lessons to heart, but many kids choose to discover "what it's like" for themselves (see #34). When they choose a course of action and the resulting experience is unpleasant, they can learn to make different and, ultimately, better choices in the future. This is experiential learning.

One important exception to the principle of using natural consequences: Natural consequences are generally preferable *unless* they pose a risk to anyone's health or safety. For example, if your kids don't like wearing seat belts, you wouldn't allow them to experience the natural consequences of that choice. A similar exception would be if the natural consequences of your child's action might seriously affect their or someone else's future (e.g., committing a crime). The key point here is just to think ahead and ask yourself whether the natural consequences would be a beneficial learning experience for your child.

Allowing children to experience the natural consequences of their choices can also minimize power struggles (#61), since you don't intervene. For example, if your son insists on wearing a T-shirt to school on a day that you find cold enough for a parka, consider letting him do so instead of getting into a power struggle about bringing his coat. If he gets cold during recess, he can go back inside, and if he doesn't want that to happen again, he's likely to make a different choice about the coat next time.

Similarly, if your son often forgets his homework (and then you drop it off at school for him), you might stop doing that and let him experience the natural consequences of forgetting his homework. If you decide to make this change, first let him know in advance (see #35) that you won't be doing it anymore, and also consider whether he may need some coaching in how to organize his morning (see #45).

See also over-functioning (#13) and risk taking (#59).

TRY THIS: As you navigate the day with your children, look for opportunities to stand back and let them learn from their experience and mistakes (with the caveats already mentioned).

Give them a preview (#35) if you disagree with their choice or have been previously "rescuing" (#13) them from *their* choices, but let it be their choice. Also consider whether your child might need some extra support to build new skills, as with how to get organized if he keeps forgetting items when he leaves the house (see #45).

If, however, natural consequences are not an option in a given situation (e.g., they might pose a threat to someone's health or safety), then:

1. Start with empathy (see #6).
2. Give the rationale for the rule (see #46).
3. Consider using distraction, pivoting (see #65), or silliness (see #69). These are most effective with younger kids.
4. Give fair warning (#47).
5. Stage a rehearsal (#73).

One example (using steps 1 to 3 above): *"Love, I know that seat belt is uncomfortable for you and you really don't like wearing it* (empathy). *Seat belts keep us safe in the car and everyone who rides in the car has to wear one* (rationale). *Hey, let's play 'I spy.' I spy something green and round* (distraction)."

51

Great parents

give speeding tickets

HAVE YOU EVER seen those electronic speed limit signs set up alongside busy roads that estimate your speed and then inform you with a flashing number if you are going too fast? Drivers vary in their responses to those signs: Some appreciate the reminder and slow down, while others ignore it.

Kids are much the same. Some kids need only a reminder that their behavior is crossing a line in order to make a change; the flashing reminder is enough. However, some kids are like those drivers who ignore the flashing sign and speed right on by: For these kids, behavior is more likely to change if they get a speeding ticket (plus an opportunity to practice a better behavior). A speeding ticket is a consequence.

By all means, if your child responds positively to reminders about his behavior, then stop there. But if your child ignores you when you set a limit, then he may need a speeding ticket (i.e., a consequence).

Unless it risks health or safety, kids need to experience the consequences of their actions. Consequences can help to improve judgment and facilitate learning, thereby increasing kids' ability to act autonomously. Kids who don't experience the consequences of their actions are insulated from critical learning experiences.

So how can parents use consequences in order to facilitate learning?

Natural consequences (#50) are generally the best teachers (like getting marked down in class for forgetting the homework), but many times natural consequences aren't an option, such as when a child refuses to wear a seat belt. Or sometimes the situation requires parents to step in and do something since there aren't any natural consequences, such as when our child is kicking the airplane seat in front of him and ignoring requests to stop.

If you need to create a consequence for your child, here are some guidelines. Consequences should be:

1. Meaningful (something important to the child, at that point in time, such as favorite toys or clothes). What is meaningful to one child is no big deal to another, so determining the right consequence requires you to know what's important to your child. (Note that what's meaningful to your child can and will change over time.)

2. Relevant (related to the situation, whenever possible). Relevant consequences help to resolve the problem, as with temporarily taking crayons away from a child who is drawing on the furniture instead of paper. When the situation involves a wrong done to someone else, a relevant consequence would generally also include making amends, such as offering an apology and replacing an item that was broken.

3. Proportionate to the intended offense. Avoid harsh or long consequences, which are punitive. Punitive consequences are most common when parents are angry or frustrated themselves (see #15 and #64). A punitive approach tends to backfire, since a consequence that is too severe gets kids focused on the unfairness of the consequence rather than on the lesson to be learned, and it can also impair the parent–child relationship (see #74).

As an example, imagine you are pulled over by the police for speeding, and you had been going ten miles per hour over the posted limit. You would expect a modest fine. But what if the police officer was having a really bad day, so she wrote you a ticket for $10,000? Instead of learning something constructive from this interaction (e.g., next time I'll slow down in this neighborhood), you would probably be more focused on how unreasonable this fine was (not to mention the officer who gave it).

4. Actionable (able to be enforced, and as soon as possible). The consequence should be something you *can* and *will* follow through on consistently (see also #1 and #53). Related to this, remember that immediacy is best when giving consequences (but see #66 if immediacy is not an option).

So taking your toddler's favorite stuffed animal away for a week, or grounding your teenager for a month, is not a good idea both because it's punitive (rather than focused on teaching; see #28) and because it's difficult to enforce. (Are you going to supervise your teenager at all times for a month? What if that stuffed animal helps your toddler to fall asleep?)

Consequences should *never* be related to your child's fundamental needs, such as food, shelter, and love. Remember, too, that kids respond best to positive reinforcement (see #24) so the best approach to changing behavior is to create opportunities for them to successfully practice the behavior you *do* want (see #21, 22, 45, 72, and 73).

How consequences are given is also important: Consequences should be communicated *and* enforced in a calm and matter-of-fact way (see #54).

The goal of consequences is not to punish but to facilitate learning. For this reason, making amends is often the best consequence. So if your child breaks a vase after you asked her not to throw a ball inside the house, then you might ask her to replace the vase from her savings or allowance.

For the same reason, when giving consequences, be sure to remind your child *why* she is receiving a consequence (see #46), and if relevant, discuss with her the effect her behavior has on others: *"Honey, I'm taking the ball away until tomorrow and we need to discuss how you will replace the vase you just broke. I asked you to throw the ball outside instead because there are too many breakable things inside. Now, the vase your Dad and I got on our honeymoon is broken. That makes me sad because of all the nice memories associated with it."*

A big challenge for many parents is creating consequences when there are no natural consequences at hand. Consequences in some situations are easier to imagine, such as taking crayons away for drawing on the furniture. Other situations are more challenging; for example, if your child is behaving inappropriately at a special event. The obvious consequence would be to leave the event, but perhaps you don't want to or cannot leave (or, in fact, leaving might be exactly what your child is hoping for). In this case, you might need to create a consequence that is meaningful to him, such as losing use of his train set for a day.

I advise parents to plan in advance, during a calm moment, a handful of meaningful consequences that are appropriate for their child. That way you have already determined several possible consequences you can draw from and are not trying to think of something in the heat of the moment, when your anger or frustration with your child's behavior can impair your ability to be fair-minded or think creatively (see also #49).

Finally, remember that consequences can suppress undesirable behavior, but parents must also tell kids what kind of behavior they'd like to see instead (#22), and then give them opportunities to practice it.

TRY THIS: *"Sweetie, I know it's boring to sit still for such a long time and you'd really like to get up and run around* (empathy). *At the same time, this is your aunt's wed-*

ding and it's very special to her (reason), *so we need to use our nicest manners even though it's hard. Let's pretend to be statues and see how still we can sit* (request with reframing; see #67). *I'm going to be a statue of a lion; what kind of statue are you? Ready, set, go!"*

If your child is capable of sitting still, but continues to squirm: Briefly repeat the rule and rationale as above, then add, *"If you choose not to sit still, then your new train set will be taken away until tomorrow* (fair warning, #47)."

Remember that we can't expect kids to follow rules and other behavior guidelines if they have not yet developed the skills to do so. If an infant starts fussing during a wedding, this is not misbehaving, and there is nothing to do but take him out of the room and calmly try to soothe him.

52

Great parents
create speed bumps

WHILE KIDS SOMETIMES need "speeding tickets" (#51) to facilitate learning (see #28), the best approach is often avoiding the problematic situation altogether. Metaphorically speaking, if you don't want your child to speed (i.e., misbehave), then create speed bumps to keep her from speeding so there is no need for a ticket. Change the environment to avoid the situation that can result in problematic behavior.

Imagine that every time you go to the grocery store, your child runs around and creates havoc. You might consider whether it's feasible to shop at another time without your child. Similarly, if your child continually takes fragile items out of a cabinet, keep the cabinet locked. Help your child behave well.

This "speed bump" strategy works best with situations that are possible to control or that are infrequent. If, however, the situation that causes the problem is part of everyday life or would be difficult for you to control, then it's probably better to invest your time and effort in changing the problematic behavior directly. (How? See #45, 46, 47, 51, 53, 72, and 73.)

TRY THIS: Observe the situations in which your child tends to misbehave. Is there a way to change the situation so that the conditions associated with the problematic behavior can be avoided?

A common example with younger children is difficulty sharing favorite toys when friends come over to play. Rather than standing by to intervene before the grabbing or hitting begins (or having to discipline your child after), you might instead ask your child to put away her special toys before her friends arrive.

"Honey, Julia and Charlotte are coming over soon. If there are any special toys that you wouldn't want them to play with, let's go put them away now. Whatever toys are still out when they arrive will be the ones everyone can play with."

Similarly, if you discover that your child has been sneaking away with your smartphone to play video games after screen time is over, instead of giving consequences each time, put a new password on your phone so he can't access it without permission.

53

Great parents
are consistent

CONSISTENCY MEANS DOING what you say you will do; it means being predictable. When we are consistent, testing of boundaries is minimized since children learn that we mean what we say and will follow through.

The principle of consistency is also key to the effectiveness of consequences (see #51). If kids perceive that you only sometimes enforce the rules, they are likely to keep testing (see also #1 and #34).

Bottom line: Don't make rules or give consequences that you can't (or won't) enforce. (But remember that rules should be reasonable and consequences should not be harsh or punitive; see #28.)

We parents aren't perfect, though (see #12), so we may not follow through 100 percent of the time. Just know that the more consistent you are with your kids, the less they will test your rules and boundaries.

For example, if we sometimes insist that our kids clear their plates from the table, and other times we are too tired or distracted to enforce this household rule, then our inconsistency effectively motivates kids to keep trying until they get the response they want.

Psychologists call this "variable ratio reinforcement." In variable ratio reinforcement, an unpredictable response motivates more attempts to get the desired outcome. Think of a rat pushing a lever that delivers food pellets. If that lever delivers food pellets at predictable (or fixed) intervals, the rat knows exactly when it will get food: every nth time it pushes the lever. The rat won't expect food at other times.

However, if the lever delivers pellets at unpredictable (or variable) intervals, the rat doesn't know if it will get food after one push, fifty pushes, or one thousand pushes, so it keeps pushing the lever again and again in the hopes that this time, it will finally get the pellet. Kids aren't rats, of course, but the principle of variable ratio reinforcement affects people, too.

Being inconsistent typically happens for one of three reasons:

1. Parents aren't paying attention (so they don't notice they have just been inconsistent).
2. Parents don't want to enforce the consequence (often because it's inconvenient or uncomfortable for them).
3. Parents can't enforce the consequence (because it's not possible or within their control).

For example, consider a scenario in which Dad is grocery shopping with his toddler, who keeps pulling items off the shelves. Dad might say, without thinking ahead: "Please stop doing that, or we will leave the store." The toddler might eye Dad mischievously while taking one more thing off the shelf. (Notice, too, that Dad also didn't give a reason—see #46—or try to redirect the behavior—see #21 and #22.)

Now Dad is faced with abandoning an almost finished shopping trip, and he can hardly be blamed for wanting to avoid that. Still, it's better for him to specify a consequence that he can and will enforce. (That said, what should Dad do in that situation if he already said the consequence would be leaving the store? I'd suggest he leave the store right away, but ask the manager to save the shopping cart for a few hours. He can return for it later or ask someone else to pick it up.)

Similarly, when we tell a child who is refusing to leave a store or playground, "Okay, 'bye. I'm leaving now and you'll have to stay here by yourself if you don't come," we are playing a game of chicken. What if the child calls our bluff and still refuses to come? We can't actually leave him there alone, so this is a poor choice of consequence since it can't be safely enforced.

TRY THIS: Pay close attention to the specific consequence you are about to communicate to your child. Better yet, consider consequences in advance, when your thinking is not impaired by strong emotions, and be sure that you can and will enforce it. Refer to #51 for guidance on how to give consequences.

If you think that you can't or won't follow through, then give a different consequence, use a placeholder (#66), or ignore the bad behavior if it's minor.

And what if you want to change your mind without appearing to be inconsistent? Be transparent about your thought process and describe why you are making a change (see #48). This will minimize the chance that your kids will mistakenly attribute your change of heart to some misbehavior on their part (such as whining, nagging, or throwing a tantrum).

54

Great parents
strive to be matter-of-fact

ONE OF THE most common parenting challenges is staying calm and matter-of-fact when kids are pushing our buttons—or anytime our reserves of patience are low. Every parent, including me, struggles with this.

Parents know they will be more effective if they are matter-of-fact, focus on feelings (#6), avoid power struggles (#61), and lovingly but firmly enforce household rules (#25). But of course this is easier said than done.

In the heat of the moment, it can be difficult to manage our own emotions so that we can effectively deal with the situation at hand, whether it's our toddler tossing his plate off the table (again) or our teenager breaking her curfew (again).

When we are feeling angry or frustrated with our kids, a common reaction is yelling or other aggressive behavior. This can feel scary and threatening to kids, or even be dramatic and interesting (see #70). In either case, letting our anger or frustration take over can change a situation from bad to worse, and it can also have longer-term consequences for our kids and our relationship with them.

Yelling may appear to get kids' attention but it's problematic because it contributes to a dysfunctional pattern of communication (see #4). Research has also shown that yelling can have harmful effects on children comparable to physical punishment, such as hitting. Children whose parents are verbally aggressive also exhibit lower self-esteem, higher aggressiveness, and increased rates of depression.[25]

It's entirely normal to feel angry or frustrated when we are dealing with our children's challenging behavior. At the same time, it's important to be careful about *how* we express those feelings. If we get highly emotional when we are dealing with our children's challenging behavior, we are likely to communicate those strong feelings, such as anger or frustration, not only through our words, but also nonverbally (#30 and #31) through body language and tone of voice, with sometimes harmful effects. Just as we are asking our kids to feel their feelings and choose their actions (#11), so must we strive to do the same.

To be clear, I am not suggesting that parents shouldn't *feel* angry or frustrated when our children misbehave, just that we shouldn't *act* on those feelings impulsively. We can feel angry without yelling or withdrawing. We can feel angry and still respond matter-of-factly.

TRY THIS: When kids are pushing your buttons or you feel that your patience is wearing thin, take a deep breath (or several) and try this technique: Pretend that you are a hotel concierge.

When we picture a concierge, most of us imagine a friendly and helpful person who can muster great reserves of restraint and calm even in challenging situations. Visualizations like this are helpful because they use the power of our imagination to rehearse a desired behavior. They prime us to act in ways that follow what we have imagined.

Here's an example: Your six-year-old son has just emerged from his room, still wearing his pajamas, even though you've already asked him several times to get dressed for school. This has also happened on several other mornings recently.

Maybe you didn't get enough sleep last night and before you can stop yourself, you yell at him: "Go change your clothes right now! This is ridiculous! I can't believe you can't just go get dressed after I've reminded you a hundred times!" This approach is likely to start a power struggle with your son, not to mention putting a damper on the morning.

So how might a concierge handle this situation? *"Sweetie, I know you really love those pj's and you wish you could wear them to school* (empathy). *At the same time, please remember that we keep our pajamas for wearing at home* (reason, #46). *Please go change for school now* (request). *Why don't you leave your pajamas here by the front door and you can change into them as soon as you get home from school* (alternative, #22)."

Although every situation is different, pretending to be a concierge can help you to act calmly and matter-of-factly—even if you're not feeling calm—by providing a model of how to approach a situation in a way that minimizes conflict and distress.

That said, if you find yourself struggling often to control your temper, know that one of the primary culprits is sleep deprivation. Lack of sleep can significantly impair our ability to control our impulses and manage our emotions. So make sure you are getting enough sleep, which for most adults is seven to nine hours each night. (See also #64.)

55

Great parents

teach happiness habits

(and also practice them)

I HAVE YET to meet a parent who doesn't want his or her kids to be happy. But parents' ideas of how to help kids be happy is often contrary to what decades' worth of research shows really works to promote well-being.

To summarize this important research, happiness has three main dimensions, or "flavors": pleasure, engagement, and meaning.

Pleasure is the kind of happiness many parents pursue for themselves and their children. The focus of pleasure is gratifying desires and preferences—for example, having delicious food, fun experiences, and beautiful things. We try to pick summer camps our kids will "like," offer them meals they "like," organize playdates with kids they "like," and so on. Over time, these repeated interactions can send kids the message that happiness is found in feeling good, having fun, and getting what they want.

While pleasure and gratification can provide a short-term happiness boost, it doesn't last long. If we want our kids to have the best chance of experiencing a happy and fulfilling life, then we must teach them how to balance their preferences with what's important, good, and meaningful. Research into the foundations of happiness shows that it is the other two qualities of activities that promote long-term happiness: engagement and meaning.

Engagement is the creative application of our skills to meet challenges. These activities often result in "flow," a state of total absorption in what we are doing.[26] Music and sports are common examples, but engagement can result from any activity that requires us to work at our full capacity, matching our skills to the challenge at hand.

Importantly, the activities most likely to create engagement are not always "fun" or pleasurable to do, at least at the outset. Like learning to play an instrument or program a computer, these types of activities are often complex and require us to develop our skills through practice and persistence (see #56).

Meaning, also defined as "service," is using our abilities to contribute to the greater good. When we strive for meaning, we are focused on pursuits that have a broader impact and purpose than our own personal goals and desires. Caring and compassion are an integral part of meaningful projects.

The bottom line? Engagement and meaning make us happier and more satisfied with life than pleasure does, and meaning contributes to the happiness of others as well. Engagement and meaning are happiness habits.

Another key happiness habit is gratitude. Gratitude is counting your blessings, whatever they may be. Practicing gratitude alleviates anxiety and depression and improves mental, emotional, and physical health. According to Robert Emmons, a prominent gratitude researcher, gratitude also strengthens relationships—the number one contributor to happiness—"because it requires us to see how we've been supported and affirmed by other people."

A fourth key happiness habit that is often overlooked as such is exercise. Exercise is a physical activity with innumerable benefits for our mental health. People who exercise are not just healthier, they are also happier. Exercise has such a profound effect on physical and mental health that it may be the single most important thing we can do to promote our well-being.[27]

Other lists of happiness habits might also include forgiveness, mindfulness, optimism, and kindness, but I've prioritized these four—engagement, meaning, gratitude, and exercise—because they promote other happiness habits and because they are balanced between making the most of ourselves (engagement and exercise) while also focusing on our relationships and communities (gratitude and meaning).

TRY THIS: Starting with these four key happiness habits, write down how you will incorporate them into your and your children's daily life. What follows are ideas for helping your kids develop these habits, but remember that if you don't also model these habits in your own life, it is less likely that your children will embrace them.

1. Engagement: Does your child have a hobby or other activity that she loses herself in (i.e., a flow activity)? Can this activity become increasingly challenging as your child's skills improve? These two qualities—a sense of timelessness while doing the activity and the possibility for an increasing level of challenge to match growing skills—are the hallmarks of engaging activities.[28]

For young children, play is a flow activity. Make sure their daily schedule allows for free and unstructured playtime (see #57). For older children (seven and up), help your child identify another engaging activity that she can learn and grow with, if she hasn't already shown an interest in something on her own. Music and sports are good starting points, but consider any activity that requires skill and provides increasing challenge, such as art, gardening, or carpentry. Be sure to keep making time for play, too.

Keep in mind that (1) your child should take the lead in identifying a flow activity and (2) your child's flow activity may not be what you had in mind. You might want baseball to be the activity your son finds engaging, but what he actually loves to do is sewing.

2. Meaning: Encourage your child to think about

the world around her. Volunteering is one excellent way to cultivate meaning, but any activity that demonstrates caring and kindness will do. This could be picking up litter in your neighborhood, donating food to a local shelter, or writing a letter to your local politician to urge action on a pressing social issue.

Keep in mind that the point of volunteering and other meaningful activities is not to build a college résumé—if your child perceives that the ultimate goal of serving others is to enhance her college application, this changes the activity from serving others to being self-serving.

3. Gratitude: One popular method of helping children develop the habit of gratitude is by incorporating it into a family meal every day. At dinner, for example, you could go around the table and ask each family member to specify one or more things he or she was grateful for that day (e.g., "I'm grateful that the sun was out today and I got to eat lunch outside" or "I'm grateful that Dad packed me my favorite snack for school today").

Some other ways to cultivate gratitude are thanking someone (in person or in a letter), keeping a gratitude journal, and praying.

4. Exercise: Exercise should be a part of your and your children's lives every day, but it does not have to involve a gym or even be called exercise.* For kids, exer-

---

* Note that the CDC recommends at least sixty minutes of exercise a day for children and adolescents.

cise should be playing. If kids are moving their bodies and getting a little sweaty, that counts.

Since there are only so many hours in a day, prioritize sleep (#58) and exercise/play over screen time or other activities.

Keep TVs and other screens on the periphery of family life. If screens are easily accessible (e.g., on a huge wall in the family room) or part of daily family life (e.g., the TV goes on during, or right after, dinner every night), then screens are likely to take up time better spent talking, playing, reading, and so on. Use screen time deliberately and purposefully. For example, you could have family movie night on Fridays or a video game competition on the weekend after a family hike.

56

Great parents
teach kids the three Ps

MANY PARENTS TELL their kids, "You can do anything!" Of course we want to encourage our children to pursue their interests and not be limited by society's view of their capabilities. At the same time, telling kids that they can do anything is not really truthful and may have unexpected downsides.

It's not true, for example, that anyone can be a professional basketball player or a fashion model, and not everyone can win a Nobel Prize or be a Supreme Court justice. We are all limited in particular ways by our genetic endowment and by the statistical realities of competition. In addition, luck and chance play a much larger role in life outcomes, including success, than we often acknowledge.[29]

In addition, research shows that when we create very ambitious goals for ourselves, those goals can become harmful—for example, leading to unethical behavior in order to meet those ambitious goals[30] or leading us to feel like a failure when we don't achieve them.

Telling kids that they can do anything creates the

vision without the road map: It implies they should set a lofty goal but gives no information about how to achieve it. Better to acknowledge that significant accomplishments will be challenging to achieve, that luck plays a key role in life, and give kids a road map for the part they can play in advancing their goals. I call this road map "the three Ps."

So instead of telling kids they can do anything, teach them the three Ps: practice, patience, and perseverance.

1. Practice, because effort coupled with feedback is critical to developing mastery and achieving excellence.
2. Patience, because mastery and meaningful accomplishment happen over a long time frame.
3. Perseverance, because obstacles are likely and setbacks are common in any endeavor.

Emphasize to your kids that success is defined by effort (see #42) and step-by-step progress, not by comparison with others. As Thomas Edison supposedly said, after a colleague discovered Edison at his workbench surrounded by the results of thousands of hours' worth of failed experiments: "I've tried everything. [But] I have not failed. I have just found ten thousand ways that won't work!"

TRY THIS: Imagine your child is struggling with science homework and exclaims in frustration: "I can't do this!" Rather than respond, "Yes, you can, let me show you," you might say something like this instead: *"Yes, science can be challenging so it's normal that you're struggling with it right now. The more time and effort you spend on it, the easier it will get."* Then support your child by answering his questions about the work as best you can, without giving him the answers (see #45).

Similarly, when you see someone who demonstrates a high level of mastery or excellence, such as a professional sports player or an accomplished musician, you might say something like this: *"Wow, she is a fantastic tennis player. I'll bet she's spent many years and thousands of hours practicing."*

57

Great parents
protect playtime

FRED ROGERS, HOST of *Mister Rogers' Neighborhood* on PBS for over thirty years, famously said, "For children, play is serious learning. Play is really the work of childhood." Research bears him out: Free and unstructured playtime is absolutely critical to all aspects of children's development.[31] Play promotes healthy brain development, creativity, decision-making skills, problem-solving skills, and social skills, just to name a few benefits.

While there are some children whose dire circumstances (such as neighborhood violence) prevent them from enjoying enough playtime, even children who live in more fortunate circumstances may not have enough time or opportunities for play. Paradoxically, affluent parents who have the means to provide free and unstructured playtime for their children are often the very ones who inadvertently deprive their children of this critical developmental experience.[32]

When children's schedules fill up with sports, tutoring, enrichment, and other structured activities—wholesome though they may be—those activities diminish the amount of time for play. In some families, playtime is whatever is left over (if anything) after other, supposedly more edifying activities have been completed. But playtime should actually be the priority. By playtime, I mean unstructured, imaginative, kid-directed play that has no external goal, but is an end in itself.[33]

This is not to say that you shouldn't get your children involved in sports, music, or other structured activities, just that you should also make every effort to ensure that they have daily opportunities for self-directed, unstructured play or free time, including outdoor time. How much time? Research suggests about sixty minutes per day at minimum, but this total time can be accrued in smaller blocks of time throughout the day.[34]

For very young kids (kindergarten age and younger) play should be their primary activity every day. If your kids are in a preschool, the preschool should be play based, meaning that the school does not have any explicit academic agenda for the kids, such as teacher-instructed prereading or math skills. Kids in play-based preschools may sometimes learn those skills through their play and interactions with teachers, but if that happens it's coincidental to the primary goals of the school, which should be to create an environment that facilitates learning and to nurture children's social and emotional development.

Kids who have the most opportunities for play also tend to develop greater self-control and executive functioning—skills that are highly correlated with future achievement.[35] (See also #33.)

TRY THIS: If your child is or will be going to a preschool, check that the preschool has a play-based philosophy, emphasizing the development of social and emotional skills over academics.

Once your child enters elementary school, check that the school offers at least one daily recess period of at least twenty minutes. These recess periods should be above and beyond any physical education (PE) classes, which are structured and adult directed. If you need after-school care for your child, prioritize options that allow her plenty of time for the kind of play described here.

Outside of school, resist the urge to schedule your child into numerous after-school activities and/or enrichment classes. How much is too much? First, make sure that activities are not impinging on your children's sleep needs (see #58). After that, experts like David Elkind recommend that time devoted to extracurricular activities not exceed the time available to children for self-directed, unstructured play.[36]

58

Great parents
prioritize sleep

In addition to playtime (#57), another critical developmental need of children is adequate sleep. However, as children's schedules get busier and school becomes more demanding, sleep is often the activity that gets shortchanged. In order to make time for soccer practice or homework or socializing, kids go to bed later and later, cutting into vital sleep time. Parents vow to do better the next night, but life gets in the way.

You may be wondering why a book focused on children's social and emotional development is highlighting a physical need like sleep, but sleep has such a powerful impact on children's mental and emotional well-being that it more than deserves mention here.

Just to name a few of the many consequences of sleep deprivation, kids who don't get enough sleep are more emotionally volatile, perform worse in school, and exhibit more behavior problems. Despite this, according to a National Sleep Foundation poll, parents often judge that their children are getting adequate sleep when in fact they are not.

The time difference between good sleep and not enough sleep is shockingly small: Researchers can detect significant behavioral and emotional improvements in kids whose sleep time is extended by just twenty-seven minutes.[37] Every minute counts.

P.S. Sleep time is also vital for adults (see #64) and can greatly affect our ability to respond calmly and matter-of-factly (#54) to our children. When a patient of mine tells me that she wants to stop yelling at her kids, one of my first questions will always be: How much sleep are you getting? There is a direct connection between sleep and the sort of impulse control needed to stop ourselves from yelling.

TRY THIS: Consider your child's sleep to be an essential, nonnegotiable activity. If there aren't enough hours in the day, then something else—not sleep—has to give.

Use these recommended sleep guidelines from the National Sleep Foundation as a starting point:

- Toddlers (ages 1 to 2): 11 to 14 hours of sleep per night
- Preschool-aged children (ages 3 to 5): 10 to 13 hours
- Elementary and middle school children (ages 6 to 13): 9 to 11 hours
- Teens (ages 14 to 17): 8 to 10 hours

Despite these recommendations, keep in mind that some kids may need slightly more or even less sleep. Use your child's behavior and emotional well-being to guide adjustments. What looks like a behavioral problem is often just a symptom of sleep deprivation.

59

Great parents
encourage sensible risk taking

IT'S NATURAL FOR parents to want to protect their children from harm of any kind, but this desire has notable downsides when applied indiscriminately. Whether we hover in the playground, forbid all tree climbing, or insist on walking our ten-year-old child down the street to a neighbor's house, we must be sure that our caution does not inhibit our children's developmental need to test their skills, learn from their mistakes, and develop resilience and perseverance.[38] Risk taking is a critical part of children's development.

The key is to balance our evaluation of potential risks with a clear-eyed assessment of potential benefits. The question we must ask ourselves is not "Is this risky?" but "Does the risk of this activity outweigh the benefits?" We can also factor into our thinking how probable and serious those potential risks are.

So if our child wants to climb a tree in the park, we might recognize that, although she might fall onto the dirt patch below, she will also learn about balance, strength, limits, and persistence. If, on the other hand, the tree in question is poised over a pile of jagged rocks, we might redirect her to a different tree, where the risk of serious injury from falling is less. Same benefits, reduced risk.

We can also tell our child why we are suggesting a different tree, so she can begin learning how to make her own sensible choices about risks and benefits. (See also #13.)

TRY THIS: What are the activities that you consider risky for your child? Which activities are off-limits or highly supervised? Consider the potential benefits of those activities for your child, from a learning and development perspective. Consider both the short-term and long-term risks and benefits. (See also #50.)

For example, you may be hesitant to allow your ten-year-old to walk down the block to his friend's house, because of the potential dangers of errant cars and menacing strangers. What are the benefits of him actually doing this? Your son develops greater autonomy from navigating his neighborhood and increases his sense of being capable, plus you don't have to supervise him every time he wants to go.

Risks? Consider the likelihood that he will be hit by a car or accosted by a stranger in your particular neighborhood. Finally, ask yourself if you can do anything to reduce some of the potential risk (as with proposing a different climbing tree in the earlier example). For instance, you could ask him to pay attention to his sur-roundings as he walks (e.g., no phones or video games) and rehearse with him what to do if a stranger ap-proaches him.

The final decision is ultimately up to you, but if you've gone through these steps it's more likely that your child will learn to take sensible risks and reap the benefits.

60

Great parents

encourage their kids to "do good"

By proposing that parents encourage their kids to "do good" I am not referring to improving their prowess in schoolwork or athletics. I am referring to children's moral education.[39]

Doing good means teaching kids to be aware of and care for the needs of others, in their families, communities, and broader society. This could mean volunteering in the local soup kitchen or befriending an unpopular kid at their school.

Doing good benefits both our children and the people they help, since children's ability to care for others directly influences their ability to lead full and satisfying lives. In addition to the benefits for both doer and receiver, kindness has a positive impact on people who merely witness it.

Doing good is also a key happiness habit (see #55), but I have made it a separate item to emphasize its importance.

TRY THIS: You can encourage your children to "do good" by modeling for them the importance of caring for others beyond their family and friends, and by spending time together doing activities that contribute to the greater good.

This can include structured activities like volunteering, or less-structured activities like skipping a meal out and donating that money to a local charity. You could pay the toll for the car behind you or smile at a stranger, and your child can invite the new kid at school to eat lunch with him or pick up trash in the local park. The amount of time that you spend on these sorts of activities will implicitly communicate how important you consider them to be.

Doing good is not for résumé building. If kids get the message, directly or indirectly, that the ultimate goal of caring for others is to advance their college admissions chances or their career, this instrumental approach will short-circuit the benefits.

61

Great parents
avoid power struggles

WE'VE ALL BEEN there: What starts as a simple request to our child ("Please put on your shoes/get ready for bed/finish your homework") is met with resistance ("No!") or simply ignored. Now what?

We can let it go or, in some cases, just do it ourselves, but that approach risks teaching our children that they can ignore our requests (see #23). We could yell at them that they had better do it *right now*, but that approach can aggravate the situation, lead to a power struggle, and impair our relationship with them (#74).

A better option would be to ask again (but see #29) and be prepared to matter-of-factly (#54) enforce our (reasonable) request with an appropriate consequence (see #51).

If the issue is important or ongoing (e.g., your son always resists getting dressed in the morning for school), then rehearsals (#73) are the best option.

However, if we are frequently using consequences in order to get our children to listen and cooperate, then it's likely that our relationship with them will suffer (or it has already). So while consequences are part of every parenting toolkit, they shouldn't be used to address every situation.

If we get into a power struggle with our children, no one wins. Better to avoid power struggles altogether.

TRY THIS: The following practices in this book can help you to avoid power struggles with your children by creating a relationship with them based on mutual trust and respect.

1. Pivot (#65): Say yes instead of no, without changing your message.
2. Reframe (#67): Use the power of imagination and play to encourage the behavior you would like to see.
3. Share your power (#37): Give kids age-appropriate opportunities to make their own choices (and mistakes).
4. Respect their reality (#8): Allow kids to think, feel, and experience the world in their own way, even when you don't understand or agree.
5. Let kids make mistakes (#13): Understand that mistakes are essential life experiences that teach kids how to do better and allow them to practice new skills.

6. Give a reason (#46): Consider the rationale for your rules and model the importance of using good reasons to motivate behavior.
7. Practice empathy (#6): Respect their feelings as they are and create a safe space for kids to experience hard feelings.
8. Maintain a warm and caring relationship (#39 and #74): Make sure your daily interactions with kids are building a loving relationship based on trust and respect.

62

Great parents

avoid reward economies

"Reward economy" is a term I coined for the arrangements that many parents make with their children to motivate "good" behavior, such as paying for chores or routinely using sticker charts that trade good behavior for prizes or rewards (even if the reward is something wholesome like books). I call them reward economies because they can create a transactional system in which children learn to trade their desirable behavior for a reward.

The problem with reward economies is not that they don't usually work to produce the desired behavior—if you have the right reward, these systems often appear to work well. As research has shown, the problem is that, over time, reward economies may negatively affect children's motivation[40] and may also create an expectation in children that they should be compensated for activities that are part of being a responsible and helpful member of the family.[41]

One telltale sign that you've inadvertently created a reward economy in your family: When you ask your kids to do something outside of their regular tasks and to-dos, such as *"Please go fold the laundry,"* and they reply, *"What will you give me?"* Another sign: You tell them you'll give them a reward/prize/sticker if they do something like helping to clean the kitchen, and they respond, *"No, thanks,"* and don't feel obliged to help since they aren't accepting the "compensation" you are offering.

Although sticker charts and similar systems seem like a good solution in the short term—we get helpful and cooperative behavior—in the long term we may be inadvertently creating a bigger problem: children who see their role in the family as a job for which they receive compensation. Moreover, reward economies often don't give children many opportunities to develop self-discipline and self-mastery, which are critical life skills (see #33).

You might be wondering what could possibly be motivating about many of the things we ask our kids to do: homework, chores, etc. My response is this: Kids who learn how to do what needs to be done—even if they don't feel like doing it—develop a strong sense of autonomy, competence, and self-mastery. There are similar benefits for kids who learn how to stop themselves from doing something desirable in the here and now in order to achieve an even more desirable future outcome (e.g., delayed gratification, as with the well-known "marshmallow" study summarized in #33).

With practice and support (#32), kids can learn how

to feel their feelings and choose their actions (#11)—for example, "I don't really want to sweep the floor right now, but I'll do it anyway because it needs to be done."

These kids are more likely to grow up to become adults who also demonstrate self-mastery. Think of how many worthwhile activities in our own lives we have delayed or skipped because we just didn't feel like doing it ("I should go to the gym tonight but I'd really rather watch this TV show/go out to dinner/finish this report").

Implementing this principle in your family may require that you trade some time and convenience in the short term for the longer-term benefit (#4) of raising children with two important traits:

1. They can do what needs to be done even when they don't feel like doing it (such as chores and studying).
2. They know how *not* to do something that they feel like doing (such as impulsive behavior).

To my mind, this is a very worthwhile trade-off, even though in the short term family life will likely run less smoothly and efficiently.

TRY THIS: Sticker charts and other reward-based systems can be used successfully but there are a number of potential pitfalls when used incorrectly, as they often are, so most parents would do better in the long run to rely on other methods to encourage good behavior.* This book is intended to provide you with those tools.

If you currently use sticker charts or similar reward systems, and you decide to stop, start by letting your kids know that you are going to make that change.† If they are in the middle of earning something important to them, let them finish and get their prize (that is, follow through on the commitment you made to them when you offered the incentive; see #1).

Your primary tools for rewarding good behavior going forward will be your acknowledgment and praise (see #24 and #42). For tasks your kids don't like or don't want to do, use empathy (#6), reason (#46), and especially rehearsals (#73).[42]

If your kids seem to ignore you when you make a request, first be sure they have actually heard you (see #29). Give them a reason to go with your request and, if you have to ask a second time, add fair warning of consequences (#47). Other useful tools are scaffolding (#45) and rehearsals. You may also have to be more involved in following up.

---

* However, there are some cases, such as children with special needs, in which reward charts are an important and necessary tool for parents.

† Sticker charts, however, can be used to good effect as a simple tracking chart, to help kids visualize their to-dos and track their progress. The key difference between a reward chart and a tracking chart is that the latter does not involve earning rewards. So kids might put a sticker on their chart to show that they finished cleaning their room, with the sticker being just a satisfying visual symbol of completion. Tracking charts do not have the same potential pitfalls as reward charts.

For example: *"Sweetie, in five minutes, it will be time to clean up your toys in the living room."* *"Noooo . . . I don't want to."* *"I know you don't want to, honey. You wish you could just keep playing* (empathy). *At the same time, we all share the house, so you need to do your part to keep it clean* (request/reason)." *"Nooo . . ."* (Or silence/ignoring.)

Now go over to your child and try to involve her in cleaning up. Try reframing (#67) to make the activity more appealing (e.g., sing a cleanup song or have a cleaning contest). If she still refuses to help, matter-of-factly (#54) restate your request, and then give fair warning of consequences (#51).

"Honey, it's time to clean up now. I know you would rather leave your toys on the floor. If you don't help clean up, then I will keep the toys that I find in the living room for [insert appropriate time frame for your child's age] *since you aren't being responsible for them* (fair warning)."

If necessary, follow through on your consequence of keeping the toys for the time you specified.

To avoid a repeat of this situation in the future, stage a rehearsal with your child in which she will practice cleaning up in a "pretend" scenario.

If she does help, be enthusiastic and specific in your praise: *"Look, we did it and the living room looks so organized! Even though you didn't want to clean up, I'm really proud of you for being a helper and putting all your cars in the box."* Remember to praise your child for any part that she did well, even if she didn't meet all your expectations. Praise reinforces good behavior.

63

Great parents

make time to give kids their full attention

A RECENT RESEARCH study showed that over one-third of working parents feel busy *all the time*.[43] At the same time, our computers and smartphones often keep us tied to whatever work or activities we are involved in. We have all seen (and probably also been) the parent who is checking e-mail or talking on the phone while our child plays nearby.

While we are fulfilling our commitments to work and other activities, we must also be sure to set aside time just to be with our kids. If we wait until we "find" the time or "have" the time, we may be waiting a long time.

As with setting aside time for ourselves (see #64), we must also make time every day to give kids our full attention. If kids don't get our uninterrupted attention freely and willingly, they are likely to resort to other methods to get it (e.g., negative attention). Misbehavior and acting out are common symptoms of not getting enough positive attention.

TRY THIS: Think about your daily schedule, or get out your calendar and examine it. For each day, identify at least one chunk of time, even if it's only five minutes, when you will put aside your other activities and obligations to spend uninterrupted time with your children. If you have more than one child, you can spend time with them together, or one at a time, depending on their relationship and your family situation.

If you are very busy or tend to have a hard time stopping work, consider actually scheduling an appointment in your calendar for regular time with your kids, and honor it as if it were a meeting with your boss or most important client. Turn off your devices and put the phone on mute. Don't allow this precious time to be put off or interrupted.

64

Great parents
take care of themselves

JUST AS PARENTS need to set aside time to be fully present with their kids, they also need to set aside time for themselves.

Ongoing self-care is critical to great parenting. If you are tired, worn out, not eating well, and not spending time doing activities that are relaxing and rejuvenating to you, you will not be your best self and your reserves of patience and energy will be diminished. This depleted state makes it much more difficult to respond calmly and skillfully to the daily challenges of raising children.

Many parents do not take enough time to care for themselves for many reasons:

- They aren't aware that their lack of self-care is significantly affecting them.
- They feel guilty for taking time away from family or work for themselves.
- They believe that they don't have the time.
- They may already be so exhausted that they don't have the motivation to do it.

You may not "feel" like taking time for yourself, but it's nevertheless important that you do so anyway (see #11).

Please, take the time to establish a *sustainable* self-care routine. To do this, you must make an appointment with yourself, as you would schedule any other meeting. If you wait until you have the time, or "find" the time, it's unlikely to happen.

A good self-care routine includes, at minimum:

- Adequate sleep (most adults need at least seven hours per night)
- Healthy food
- Regular exercise (simple walking is fine)
- Regular "me" time (for solitude, a hobby, etc.)
- Regular social time (with spouse/partner and/or friends)

Having a good self-care routine not only helps you to be a better parent, it also models a healthy lifestyle for your kids.

The "routine" aspect of a good self-care routine is also critical. You will have a greater likelihood of success if you decide in advance specifically when and how you will exercise, meet friends, meditate, go to sleep, and so on.

Following a specific and established routine instead of revisiting these decisions every day will free up energy to focus on other priorities (e.g., "I will take a walk every Monday, Wednesday, and Friday during my lunch hour," or "When my daughter is napping/at soccer practice, I will meditate").

Taking care of yourself also helps to teach kids that other people's needs are important and provides a positive model of adulthood. If you are constantly sacrificing your needs (e.g., sleep, leisure, time with friends, important projects, etc.) to those of your kids, they are probably not learning how to balance their needs with others'. This is a recipe for entitled kids and strained relationships. It may seem paradoxical, but reserving some of your time and energy for yourself will benefit your child.

TRY THIS: Ask yourself: Would I want my kids to copy the life habits I have now? (See also #20.)

Get out your calendar and schedule twenty to thirty minutes at least three days per week to exercise (walk around the block, hike, swim, dance in your living room, stretch, etc.). You don't have to go to a gym or class. Just move and stretch your body.

Actually write down the specific days and times when you will exercise, and block them out in your calendar. Consider exercising with a friend so that you will find it more difficult to skip (plus reap the benefits of being social).

Do the same at least once per month for a social activity (date night, lunch or coffee with friends, volunteering, etc.).

Make sure you are getting enough sleep for your individual needs. For most adults, this is about seven hours per night. You can make a good guess as to what your sleep needs are based on how long you typically sleep after several days of vacation, without using an alarm.

Please don't underestimate the negative effects of not getting enough sleep. If you struggle with depression, anxiety, or even yelling at your kids, sleep deprivation may be part of the culprit.

As you get more adept at setting aside time to take care of yourself, add in more activities and/or greater frequency as your schedule permits.

65

Great parents
pivot

PIVOTING IS THE art of saying yes instead of no, and meaning the same thing.

TRY THIS: Instead of saying *"No, we can't go to the park until after you have a nap,"* pivot and say: *"Yes, we can go to the park as soon as you're done with your nap."*

The message is the same, but the tone is completely different. Plus, saying "yes" gives kids a lot less to argue with.

66

Great parents
use placeholders

PLACEHOLDERS, AS I call them, are a useful technique that come in handy when you need to address an episode of bad behavior, but you don't have time (e.g., you have to leave for the office) or the moment is not conducive to a productive discussion (e.g., you and/or the kids are tired and/or hungry; see #27).

When you must discipline kids, immediacy is always best, but realistically, that is not always possible. In those instances, use a placeholder and return to the episode as soon as possible.

A placeholder is a brief acknowledgment that something has happened that requires attention, while noting that the discussion must be temporarily deferred.

TRY THIS: Instead of letting timing, hunger, or fatigue keep you from addressing an episode of behavior that you don't want repeated, use a placeholder and then come back to the issue as soon as time and tempers allow.

"Honey, I just saw you sneak a cookie out of the pantry even though I've told you before that you need to ask me or Dad first. We need to discuss this, but I have to leave for work right now. When I get home tonight, we'll talk about it."

Here's an example with a hungry toddler, who just threw his plate and hit you with it. *"Ouch! You just threw that plate and hit me. I think you're very hungry right now, so let's get you some food and we'll talk about what just happened after your snack."*

67

Great parents
reframe

IT OFTEN HAPPENS that parents ask kids to do something seemingly simple, like stand still or be quiet or clean up their room, and then get frustrated when it doesn't happen. There is a better way: reframing.

Reframing, as I call it, is engaging kids' imagination and sense of play in order to encourage the behavior you would like to see. This practice works best with younger children. A fascinating study of four-year-olds shows the power of this strategy.[44]

In the study, the researchers first gave kids a simple instruction: Stand still for as long as you can. The kids didn't last very long at this task—usually less than a minute. Then the researchers asked the kids to pretend that they were guards at a factory. Now the kids were able to stand still almost four times as long. Why? Because they were imaginatively engaged in the activity.

You can also see reframing at work in many preschools, when everyone sings the "cleanup song" while the kids put away toys and organize the room. Reframing helps kids be successful.

Reframing is also good practice for adults because it uses our own creativity to reframe our request ("Stand still") as a more imaginative activity ("Pretend you are guarding a factory").

TRY THIS: The next time you want your young child to do something, think of a more fun and imaginative way to describe your request, and "reframe" it.

For example, before going into an event that requires quiet, you might say to your child in a conspiratorial voice: *"I heard there might be aliens coming who are not invited. Can you please listen carefully for them so if they come, we can ask them to leave? You have to listen hard because they are very, very quiet. If you think you hear one, whisper in my ear so they won't hear you."*

What are the activities in your kids' life that often meet with resistance, and how can you reframe them more imaginatively?

See also #29.

68

Great parents

focus on the positive

A FRIEND OF mine likes to say that parents can see the future. What she means by this is that we can often sense when a situation has a high probability of going badly. For example, we see our kids playing with their drinks at the table and we may think, "That's going to spill," or we may see our child climbing a tree and think, "She's going to fall!"

It's our job as parents to help our children navigate the world, learn to make good choices, and take sensible risks. That said, it's helpful to our kids if we can phrase our concerns and teachings in a positive way. For example, we can say "Keep the milk in the cup" instead of "Don't spill." We can say "Hold on tightly!" instead of "Don't fall!"

Because words evoke ideas and images, when our kids hear "Don't fall" they are likely to conjure images of falling, which is not ideal if they are in a precarious position. When we say instead "Hold on tightly!" our intention is the same, but our words now have a more helpful focus and imagery.

Similarly, when we are trying to change "bad" behavior (e.g., whining or demanding) it is more effective to tell children what to do (e.g., "Take a big breath and say 'please' in a calm voice"), instead of telling them what not to do (e.g., "Stop whining"). (See also #22.)

The importance of focusing on the positive is also central to two other Great Parenting practices we discussed earlier in this book: how we view our kids (see #24 and #36) and how we teach them to view the world (see #55).

TRY THIS: Tell kids what *to* do, instead of what *not* to do.

Similarly, when children make, for example, a grammatical mistake, instead of pointing it out directly to them as an error ("No, it's not 'the cat go under there' it's 'the cat went under there'") we can just repeat their sentence back to them using proper grammar: "Oh, the cat went under there. I see it now." With repetition and practice, kids will learn the correct form of speech, with a minimum of self-consciousness about making errors.

For related ways to use this principle, see also #65.

69

Great parents

can change the mood (be silly and playful)

ASIDE FROM BEING fun (and good for you), being silly at the right moment can often pull kids (and us) out of a bad mood.

You'll need to consider how attached your child is to being upset, but oftentimes, if you can catch her at the right moment, you can "turn that frown upside down" by not taking the moment so seriously.

TRY THIS: If you notice that your child is starting to get grumpy or slightly upset, you might say in a part silly, part stern voice: *"Oh, you look very frustrated. Grumph. Harrumph."* As you start to notice the glimmer of a smile: *"Oh, wait, you can't smile if you're grumpy. No smiling . . . No smiling . . ."* Often, by this time, your kids will be starting to giggle.

Similarly, if your child is refusing to put on her shoes, you might try playfulness instead of discipline: *"Okay, if you don't want to wear these shoes, I'm going to wear them."* (Take her shoe, and try to put it on your foot.) *"Oops, that doesn't fit. Maybe it'll fit here."* (her shoe on your elbow). *"Nope, how about here?"* (her shoe on your nose). You get the idea. Continue until (hopefully) giggles ensue.

This practice works best with younger children. Delivery, tone, and timing are everything.

Pay close attention to how your child is responding to your early attempts to change the mood, so that you don't accidentally miss a situation in which your child is truly upset or distressed.

Be ready to shift gears quickly if the mood doesn't seem to be changing in response to your playfulness. Then go straight to empathy (see #6).

70

Great parents

avoid drama

SOMETIMES THE MOMENT calls for silliness (#69), but at other times the best strategy is to be boring. Boring is best when your child is misbehaving for attention or is trying to provoke you.

In those instances, part of the payoff for your child's provocative behavior (see #23) is the drama it creates. If you want to minimize the drama and deescalate the situation, try to be boring. This is far easier said than done.

Being boring means keeping the energy level down and not letting yourself be provoked. For example, if your child has misbehaved and, while you are giving her a consequence, she tries to provoke you further by smirking or rolling her eyes, the most effective response is often to ignore it and keep the focus on her more serious misdeed. (See also #54.)

Similarly, if your child keeps getting out of bed at night after you tuck her in, be boring as you return her to bed. Don't get pulled into conversation or drama. Keep the emotional tone as neutral as possible. If you show agitation or anger when she gets out of bed, your response becomes "interesting" and this provides more motivation for your child to keep getting up.

TRY THIS: Since bedtime struggles are so common, I'll use a bedtime scenario to illustrate being boring. It's simple (but not easy): Every time you are aware that your child has gotten out of bed, gently take her by the hand and say something like this as you return her to bed: *"It's time to sleep now. Let's go back to bed. I'll see you in the morning. Good night."* (Kiss.)

It's essential that your tone of voice and body language are also calm and boring when you say this. Tuck her back in. Repeat as needed (possibly dozens of times).

Stick to the wording you have selected and keep the interaction calm and brief. The underlying message you are trying to communicate (#31) is: "Nothing interesting will happen when you get up, so you may as well stay in bed."

If you have another adult in the house, trade off being in charge of this process so that each of you is "on" every other night. This scheduling creates predictability (see #53) and also ensures that each of you has an evening off. Remember that trying to be the bedtime enforcer every night on your own, while possible, is draining, and that sleep deprivation will make it even harder for you to remain matter-of-fact and "boring."

71

Great parents
stop the action

STOPPING THE ACTION is a powerful behavioral tool for parents. Think of it as hitting the pause button in life.

Stopping the action tells kids through your response to the situation that what is happening is not okay and that the moment or interaction will not continue as is with your participation. I have worked with many parents who have talked themselves hoarse telling kids, "It's not okay to talk to me that way," but nevertheless continue the conversation as their child continues to yell.

In those situations, parents are essentially saying one thing but doing another (see also #51). Instead, parents will get a better result by *also* stopping the action.

TRY THIS: The next time you notice your child engaged in an inappropriate or unpleasant behavior (e.g., grabbing, whining, yelling), stop the interaction and say why. After that, the next step is to ask for a replay (see #72).

For example: Your two-year-old drops his cup while sitting at the table. He yells and points down at the cup. Instead of immediately picking it up for him, pause for a moment—that's stopping the action—and ask him to take a deep breath and say please (this is a replay). When he does, pick up the cup and hand it to him. (See also #21.) Note that a replay (breathing and saying please in this example) can be any alternative behavior that is acceptable to you, and must also be something that your child can do successfully (see #22).

Another example: Your teenage daughter is getting frustrated and angry as she listens to you telling her why she can't sleep over at a friend's house that weekend. She yells at you, "You don't understand anything!" Instead of continuing the conversation and explaining to her why you actually do understand, pause and stop talking.

Explain that you are willing to discuss this issue with her, but not if she yells or is disrespectful. Ask for a replay and resume the conversation. If she yells again, stop. If it happens a third time, tell her you both need a break and you can try to talk again later (and give her a specific time or occasion, e.g., after dinner). Then matter-of-factly disengage from the conversation.

72

Great parents
offer replays

THINK OF A replay as using the rewind button to start over and play out a better scene and outcome. Replays typically follow after you "stop the action" (see #71).

A replay is essentially an opportunity to try again and do better. This is especially important with younger kids, who are engaged in serious experimentation with almost everything (see #34).

Replays are a critical part of learning. They are a chance to practice something new and get better. Replays are also an essential part of forming new habits (see #20), since the more we repeat something, the more habitual it becomes.

A replay is especially useful after a consequence has been given or after you've noticed an inappropriate behavior (such as grabbing or whining).

Before you ask for a replay, you and/or your child must identify a preferable way to handle the situation (see #22). Once you have identified a better way to proceed, the replay is acted out using that new and improved behavior, and then praised in a specific way (see #24 and #42 for guidelines).

Another practice closely related to replays is rehearsals (see #73).

TRY THIS: Here are two examples, the first based on the all-too-common situation of your toddler throwing food on the floor during a meal, the second based on an equally common situation in which your older child has just said something disrespectful.

"Jimmy, please stop throwing your peas on the floor (rule). *When you do that, it wastes food and makes a mess* (reason). *If you throw the peas again, I'm taking the bowl away* (fair warning)."* True, most toddlers will not understand everything that you're saying to them (although you may be surprised at how much they do understand). Your actions will reinforce the message. In the meantime, your discussion with them will be gradually building their language skills.

When Jimmy throws the peas again—which is likely, since he's either experimenting on you and/or the peas or he doesn't understand yet what you are telling him—then calmly and matter-of-factly take the bowl away for about ten seconds. Then give it back and let him try again (replay). Repeat as needed.

He will soon learn that the peas go away when he throws them. If he wants to eat the peas, he will stop. If he keeps playing with the peas after several replays, that's a good sign that he's done eating them.

Second example: As you are serving dinner, your daughter says in a disrespectful tone of voice: *"Mommm! You know I don't like my sauce mixed in with my pasta! Yuck!"*

Pause, stop the action, take a deep breath, and respond matter-of-factly: *"Sandy, I don't know if you can hear it* (benefit of the doubt; see #36), *but you're using a disrespectful tone of voice right now* (rule).* *I can see that there's something you don't like about dinner* (empathy; see #6), *and that's not an appropriate way to tell me* (method vs. goal; see #21). *Please try again* (replay).*"

Wait for her to rephrase her complaint in an acceptable way, or you can suggest an alternative for her (the latter works best for young children). For example: *"Sandy, if you want to tell me that you don't like something about dinner, you could say 'Mom, thanks for making dinner, but I was hoping to have my sauce separately.'"*

After a successful replay, reengage (in the previous example, give her the sauce on the side). If she does not try to use a better alternative, then tell her you will be happy to help her when she communicates more respectfully, and be sure she knows what that would sound like. (See also #23.)

---

* Do you speak to *her* disrespectfully? (See #40.)

73

Great parents

stage rehearsals

EVEN IF YOUR child has no interest in becoming a Broadway star, the world of performing arts has a useful practice that parents can borrow: the rehearsal. In parenting, as in theater, a rehearsal is a chance to practice a new behavior until it becomes more familiar and routine.

Since practice is essential to learning, when we want children to learn a new behavior, or to substitute a desirable behavior for a problematic one, we need to give kids opportunities to practice that new behavior (and then praise them in specific ways to reinforce it; see #42). Many times these opportunities for practice don't happen on their own, in which case parents can create them. This is what I mean by staging a rehearsal.

In contrast to real life, in which strong emotions, habits, and time pressures can derail attempts to behave differently, a rehearsal lets kids practice a new or substitute behavior in a setting that supports learning.

In this kind of rehearsal—just as with a dress rehearsal in the theater—you set the stage as closely as possible to simulate the real situation and then encourage your child to practice the new behavior, with the goal of having the new behavior become more familiar and accessible when "real life" happens.

So if your child habitually leaves his coat and backpack in a heap by the door when he comes home after school, you could stage a rehearsal over the weekend by asking him to walk in the door as if it were a school day, and then to hang up his coat and put his shoes and backpack in the closet. Any degree of success would be reinforced with praise.

Rehearsals are useful both for teaching new behaviors (e.g., how to greet an adult politely, how to set the table, and so on) and for encouraging kids to substitute a behavior they already know for another one that you would prefer (e.g., saying "Please may I have it?" instead of "I want it!" or getting dressed before breakfast instead of eating in pajamas so that they are more likely to leave for school on time).

Rehearsals can also be used to minimize tantrums and other problematic behaviors. For example, if your child gets physically aggressive when she's upset (e.g., hitting and throwing things) Alan Kazdin of Yale University suggests asking her to pretend to be angry or frustrated at a time when she is actually feeling calm. During this game, you would ask her to practice keeping her hands to herself while pretending to be angry and then praise her for it. If she later tries this new behavior, even in part, when she is actually feeling angry, you would also praise her for this incremental success (see #24). Instead of trying to eliminate the problematic behavior all at once (e.g., no tantrums), you would rehearse with your child the experience of being angry without hitting, then without throwing, and praise her specifically as she makes step-by-step progress. See also scaffolding (#45) and replays (#72).

TRY THIS: Let's say your son typically comes home from school and dumps his clothes, shoes, and backpack on the floor in a heap. You've asked (nagged?) him repeatedly to put everything away before he goes to play, but the old behavior persists. Stop nagging and start rehearsing.

Pick a day and time when everyone is more relaxed and there are minimal time pressures. Now set the stage to mimic real life: Ask him to put on his school clothes and give him his backpack, just as if it were a real school day.

Now ask him to walk in the door as he normally would, but instead of his usual routine (dump and go) the practice behavior is to hang up his coat and put his shoes and backpack away. Praise him sincerely, specifically, and immediately when he does.

If he doesn't get all the steps right, praise him for what he did do well: *"It's so nice to see your coat hung up neatly in the closet. Thank you! Let's try it again and this time focus on also putting your bag and shoes away."* Repeat (in multiple rehearsal sessions, if necessary) until the new behavior seems comfortable and familiar to your child.

Also, be sure to keep rehearsals positive (no criticizing if he doesn't get it right) so that he won't resist the idea of rehearsals in the future.

See also #32.

74

Great parents

focus on the relationship

YOU'VE PROBABLY HEARD the common wisdom in real estate that what matters is location, location, location. Similarly, what matters most with kids is relationship, relationship, relationship.

Without a strong, loving relationship built on mutual trust and respect, all the principles and practices described here are just techniques for increasing compliance. In the context of a good relationship, however, the ideas discussed in this book become a powerful tool for parents to create a family life that is loving, supportive, and harmonious.

When we have a good relationship with our children—a relationship characterized by empathy, patience, compassion, trust, and respect—our kids will *want* to please us and will be much more cooperative when we try to redirect their behavior and teach them positive habits. (See also #37.) A strong and loving parent–child relationship also has a significant positive influence on all aspects of children's development—social, emotional, cognitive, and physical—and is tied to favorable outcomes in almost every area of life.

This kind of positive parent–child relationship does not mean that our children are like our friends. We hopefully enjoy each other's company and spend time together, as friends also do, but ultimately we always remain our children's parents, even when they become adults.

TRY THIS: A relationship is built one interaction at a time over many thousands of moments. Observe your daily interactions with your children and ask yourself if those individual moments, when added up over decades, will create the kind of relationship you want to have. If not, use the ideas in this book to start making changes.

75

Great parents

start where they are

IF YOU'RE READING this after having read the rest of the book, you may be feeling some anxiety or regret about your past parenting. These feelings are normal; it is common to feel some anxiety or regret when we learn something we wish we could have acted on earlier.

Please keep in mind that you can only act on what you know, and most parents have been doing the best they can with what they know so far. Thankfully, most kids are both resilient and forgiving; they are more like hardy weeds than fragile flowers. Remember, too, that no parent is perfect (see #12).

More importantly, please do not allow your anxiety or regret over mistakes in the past to keep you from acting on what you know *now*. As one of my favorite proverbs reminds us: "The best time to plant a tree is twenty years ago, but the second best time is now."

I hope that this book has given you the tools and understanding to create the kind of relationship that you want with your kids, starting right now.

Notes

1. Sandra Aamodt and Sam Wang, *Welcome to Your Child's Brain*. New York: Bloomsbury, 2012.
2. Sara F. Waters, Tessa V. West, and Wendy Berry Mendes, "Stress Contagion: Physiological Covariation between Mothers and Infants," *Psychological Science* 25, no. 4 (2014): 934–42.
3. Lisa H. Albers, Dana E. Johnson, et al., "Health of Children Adopted from the Former Soviet Union and Eastern Europe: Comparison with Preadoptive Medical Records," *Journal of the American Medical Association* 278, no. 11 (1997): 922–24.
4. http://www.apa.org/monitor/2012/04/spanking.aspx.
5. http://www.sciencedaily.com/releases/2015/03/150316165949.htm.
6. An excellent book on how habits form and how to change them is Charles Duhigg's *The Power of Habit* (New York: Random House, 2014).
7. Nancy Eisenberg, "Emotion, Regulation, and Moral Development," *Annual Review of Psychology* 51 (2000): 665–97.
8. http://www.alisongopnik.com/papers_alison/sciam-gopnik.pdf.
9. http://journal.frontiersin.org/article/10.3389/fnhum.2014.00229/abstract.

10. Z. Ivcevic and M. Brackett, Predicting School Success: Comparing Conscientiousness, Grit, and Emotion Regulation Ability," *Journal of Research in Personality* 52 (2014): 29–36.

11. The concept of emotion coaching is drawn from the work of John Gottman and colleagues.

12. Wang and Aamodt, *Welcome to Your Child's Brain.*

13. Roy Baumeister research.

14. Alison Gopnick, Andrew Meltzoff, and Patricia Kuhl popularized the notion of babies and children as scientists. See their excellent book, *The Scientist in the Crib* (New York: First Perennial, 2000).

15. I thank Susan DeMersseman for her phrase "works in progress with the intent to do better."

16. S. H. Chen, Q. Zhou, et al., "Parental Expressivity in Chinese Families: Prospective and Unique Relations to Children's Psychological Adjustment," *Parenting: Science and Practice* 11, no. 4 (2011): 288–307.

17. http://www.eurekalert.org/pub_releases/2015-01/uom-cfm 012715.php.

18. http://www.ncbi.nlm.nih.gov/pubmed/20331670.

19. These parenting styles are based on the research of developmental psychologist Diana Baumrind.

20. http://newsroom.ucla.edu/releases/lack-of-parental-warmth -abuse-248580.

21. James Morehead, "Stanford University's Carol Dweck on the Growth Mindset and Education," OneDublin.org (June 19, 2012).

22. Ibid.

23. http://articles.latimes.com/1988-04-08/news/vw-1120_1_shy -child.

24. The concept of scaffolding, often used in classrooms, is based especially on the work of Jerome Bruner and Lev Vygotsky.

25. M.-T. Wang and S. Kenny, "Longitudinal Links Between Fathers' and Mothers' Harsh Verbal Discipline and Adolescents' Conduct Problems and Depressive Symptoms." *Child Development* 85 (May/June 2014): 908–923, *Journal of Marriage and Family* 65 (November 2003): 795–808.

26. For more information about the concept of flow and how to achieve it, I highly recommend Mihaly Csikszentmihalyi's seminal book *Flow: The Psychology of Optimal Experience* (New York: HarperCollins, 2008).

27. http://www.aomrc.org.uk/general-news/exercise-the-miracle -cure.html.

28. Ibid.

29. See, for example, Daniel Kahneman, *Thinking Fast and Slow* (New York: Farrar, Straus and Giroux, 2013).

30. Lisa D. Ordóñez, Maurice E. Schweitzer, et al., "Goals Gone Wild: The Systematic Side Effects of Overprescribing Goal Setting," *Academy of Management Perspectives* 23, no. 1 (2009).

31. http://pediatrics.aappublications.org/content/119/1/182.

32. For a deeper look at this issue, see Madeline Levine's excellent book, *The Price of Privilege* (New York: Harper Perennial, 2008).

33. This definition of "play" is borrowed from Peter Gray.

34. http://www.cdc.gov/physicalactivity/everyone/guidelines/chil dren.html.

35. Adele Diamond, W. Steven Barnett, et al., "Preschool Program Improves Cognitive Control," *Science* 318, no. 5855 (2007): 1397– 88.

36. An excellent resource for parents and educators interested in how to protect the well-being of kids of all ages from an overemphasis on achievement is the Challenge Success program at Stanford University. Their website is full of useful information (www.challengesuccess.org).

37. http://pediatrics.aappublications.org/content/early/2012/10/10 /peds.2012-0564.abstract?sid=365a3da0-8f51-48bf-a82a -4647e036f8e1.

38. http://www.decd.sa.gov.au/oshc/pages/default/play/?reFlag=1.

39. Richard Weissbourd has written an important book on this subject: *The Parents We Mean to Be* (New York: Houghton Mifflin Harcourt, 2010).

40. Research shows that when external incentives or rewards are offered for performing a task, those incentives decrease an individual's internal motivation. This negative effect is even more

pronounced in kids. See E. L. Deci, R. Koestner, and R. M. Ryan, "A Meta-Analytic Review of Experiments Examining the Effects of Extrinsic Rewards on Intrinsic Motivation," *Psychological Bulletin* 125, no. 6 (1999): 627–68.

41. See also http://www.theatlantic.com/health/archive/2016/02/perils-of-sticker-charts/470160/

42. Rewards can, however, be useful occasionally for helping children reach milestones (such as toilet training) or for motivating them to participate in unpleasant but necessary activities (such as getting shots at the doctor's office). The key is to avoid using rewards frequently or systematically as a way of managing the regular activities of family life, unless you are getting specific guidance from a professional to do so.

43. http://www.pewsocialtrends.org/2013/03/14/modern-parenthood-roles-of-moms-and-dads-converge-as-they-balance-work-and-family/.

44. http://www.nytimes.com/2009/09/27/magazine/27tools-t.html?pagewanted=all&_r=0.